Burns and Oates

Manual of Prayers For the Use of the Pilgrims to

Paray-le-Monial

September 2, 1873

Burns and Oates

Manual of Prayers For the Use of the Pilgrims to Paray-le-Monial
September 2, 1873

ISBN/EAN: 9783337274931

Printed in Europe, USA, Canada, Australia, Japan

Cover: Foto ©Lupo / pixelio.de

More available books at **www.hansebooks.com**

MANUAL OF PRAYERS

FOR THE USE OF THE

Pilgrims to Paray-le-Monial,

SEPTEMBER 2, 1873.

LONDON: BURNS AND OATES,

Portman Street and Paternoster Row.

PREFACE.

I.

PILGRIMAGE FROM ENGLAND TO PARAY-LE-MONIAL, IN HONOUR OF THE SACRED HEART.

AT this time, when the Church is going through a period of extraordinary tribulation in the person of the Supreme Pontiff, of her Bishops and Priests, and of the religious orders—her strength and her glory —the feeling, natural to all Christians, that in prayer alone can be found the remedy for all these evils, is now assuming a form which has been in all ages one of the most vivid expressions of Catholic Faith— that of pilgrimages to those sanctuaries where an- cient devotion or recent graces have led men to ex- claim as the Patriarch Jacob at Bethel: 'Indeed, the Lord is in this place.'

So instinctive, if we may so speak, so spontane- ous, and so rapid in its spread has been this pious impulse, that it would seem to indicate a special correspondence with the needs of the present period. The ease with which men unite for various pur- poses, the facility with which space is traversed and

thoughts transmitted in our days, has often served
the interests of Satan and his agents. The followers
of Jesus Christ are now using these means for an
opposite end. In the face of an infidel and blas-
pheming world they feel impelled openly to proclaim
their love for our Divine Lord, and to call upon Him
'who alone is great and does wonderful things' to
give ear unto their prayers. France, Germany, Italy,
Switzerland, and Belgium all share in this holy
movement. We Catholics in England propose to
take our part in it.

It will be well to make special mention of the
place which has been fixed upon as the object of our
Pilgrimage. Those who have read the life of the
Blessed Margaret Alacoque are already familiar with
the name of Paray-le-Monial; but there may be many
who do not know the reason why this small and
obscure French town is connected with the devotion
of the Sacred Heart, and why numberless pilgrims
have gone thither during the month dedicated to its
worship, to pray for their Church and for their
country; for Rome and for France.

Exactly two hundred years ago a miracle of divine love took place in the humble little Convent
of the Visitation at Paray, which opened the source
of all the graces which have flowed ever since from
the devotion to the Sacred Heart of Jesus.

To a humble daughter of St. Francis of Sales,
who had nursed in her pure and child-like soul an
ardent love to our Blessed Lord, that Divine Saviour

appeared. He saw her at prayer under a tree in the
little garden of the convent, as He once saw Na-
thaniel under the fig-tree, and to that heart that had
no guile He vouchsafed to intrust the message that
promised countless blessings to all who would honour
with a special love and devotion His Sacred Heart
—'that Heart that has loved men so much and has
been so little loved in return.'

Through good and evil report, through persecu-
tion and contempt, humbly and perseveringly, that
pure soul bore witness to the desire of her Lord, and
delivered this message of boundless love, until the
hearts of men began at last to believe in it, and to
test and to experience its truth.

The Church set her seal on this devotion; re-
cognised, proclaimed, and recommended it to the
faithful.

This year, therefore, which is the second cen-
tenary of that gracious revelation, has been chosen
as one of special appeal to the Sacred Heart of our
Lord; one so urgent, so unanimous, and so humble,
that it cannot fail to reach that Divine Heart, and
to move it to compassion; and Paray-le-Monial, the
scene of our Lord's apparition to His chosen daughter, has been selected as the most fitting place for
that appeal. It is a singular fact that it was in
London that the special devotion to the Sacred
Heart was for the first time alluded to in a public
manner. Father la Colombière, S.J., touched upon
it in a sermon which he preached on Corpus Christi,

1677, in the Chapel of St. James's, before the Duchess of York—afterwards Queen Mary Beatrice.

We have now only to add that his Grace the Archbishop of Westminster, and many of our Bishops, have given their warmest sanction and encouragement to the pilgrimage from England, and their blessing to all those who take part in it; and we would point out that this may be done in various ways. Those who cannot perform the pilgrimage themselves may enable others by their contributions to join in it, or may help to make an offering at the Shrine, or contribute to the Fund; and offerings for this purpose, as well as for the general objects of the pilgrimage, will be thankfully received by the Committee. All who help to make known and to recommend this national Catholic act of homage to our Blessed Lord will aid its success and share in its graces.

Committee.

The Duke of Norfolk.
The Earl of Denbigh.
Lord Herries.
Sir Charles Clifford.
Charles Langdale, Esq.
The Right Rev. Monsignor Capel.
The Hon. and Rev. Gilbert Talbot, D.D.
The Very Rev. Father Kirk.
The Very Rev. Father Clare, S.J.
The Rev. Father Gordon, of the Oratory.

The Marchioness Dowager of Lothian.
The Lady Georgiana Fullerton.
The Lady Herbert of Lea.
Lord Walter Kerr, Hon. Sec. (15 Bruton-street, London, W.).

II.

APPROBATION OF THE ENGLISH HIERARCHY ASSEMBLED IN PROVINCIAL COUNCIL.

To his Grace the Duke of Norfolk and others of the Faithful, the Archbishop and Bishops of England in Synod assembled.

Health and Benediction in the Lord.

As soon as it became known to us, dearly beloved son, that, with a numerous and distinguished company of the Faithful of our country, you had resolved, in honour of the Sacred Heart of Jesus, to make a pilgrimage of devotion to the relics of Blessed Margaret Mary at Paray-le-Monial, we rejoiced with our whole heart, for it seemed unworthy of the faith of our country that the name and piety of England should be unrepresented in that wonderful concourse of the Faithful, by which, in many sanctuaries of France, a resplendent testimony is now being given against the unbelief and wickedness of the world. In the cruel war which we see daily and everywhere breaking out, not only against the Church of

God, but also against the civil life of men, against
the truths of the natural order and the instinctive
laws of morality, the only safe defence for mankind
is to be found in the Most Sacred Heart of our
Redeemer. When the flood of Divine wrath which
is now threatening the world shall have come, he
that shall be in this ark shall be saved, he that
shall be found out of it shall perish. The king-
doms also and the nations which, with an obstinate
audacity, have long refused to serve God and His
Christ shall, as the Holy Spirit has foretold, be
destroyed by mutual slaughter, and by a just judgment be soon scattered like smoke before the face
of the Lord. Go then, dearly beloved son, you and
your companions, and, in the sight of this world,
which knows not how to pray, make supplication to
the most loving Heart of Jesus. Pray for our Pontiff Pius; for the whole Church throughout the
world; for the Bishops and Priests, and the Faithful of Christ, who in Germany and in Switzerland
are gloriously striving against the tyranny of un-
believers and the wickedness of destroyers; for the
nations once Christian, but which to-day are miser-
ably fallen from the faith; and, lastly, pray all of
you with earnestness for our beloved England, that
from the side of Jesus, which was opened for us
with the lance, the fulness of all sanctity and forti-
tude may flow down upon us. Giving thanks, therefore, to you and your companions for the devout
pilgrimage which, also in our name, you are about

to undertake, we lovingly and from our hearts bestow our blessing on you; and we earnestly commend you all to the loving charity of our brethren the Bishops of the Catholic Church, and of all the Clergy and Faithful, that in every good service they may be at hand to help you.

Given in the Fourth Provincial Council of Westminster on the 23d day of July 1873.

(Signed)

✠ HENRY EDWARD, *Archbishop of Westminster.*

✠ THOMAS JOSEPH, *O.S.B., Bishop of Newport and Menevia.*

✠ WILLIAM BERNARD, *O.S.B., Bishop of Birmingham.*

✠ JAMES, *Bishop of Shrewsbury.*

✠ RICHARD, *Bishop of Nottingham.*

✠ WILLIAM, *Bishop of Plymouth.*

✠ WILLIAM, *Bishop of Clifton.*

✠ FRANCIS, *Bishop of Northampton.*

✠ ROBERT, *Bishop of Beverley.*

✠ JAMES, *Bishop of Hexham and Newcastle.*

✠ JAMES, *Bishop of Southwark.*

✠ HERBERT, *Bishop of Salford.*

✠ BERNARD, *Bishop of Liverpool.*

III.

BRIEF OF THE HOLY FATHER ON THE FRENCH PILGRIMAGES.

The following is the text of the Reply of his Holiness to the Address recently presented to him on the occasion of the pilgrimages to Paray-le-Monial:

To our dear sons Lucien Brun, G. de Belcastel, Count Abbàdie de Barrau, and to all the Deputies of the National Assembly of France who, with the intention of devoting themselves to the Sacred Heart, have organised the Ceremony of Supplication at Paray-le-Monial, Lyons.

PIUS IX., POPE.

Dear Sons, Salutation and Apostolic Benediction.—We have not doubted, dearly-beloved sons, that there would rise again in France, after the long darkness of error, the Sun of Justice, so soon as we perceived that it was manifestly preceded by that joyful Aurora, the Mother of Grace. It is she who by her presence has made this nation emerge from its sleep; it is she who has gently drawn the people —she who has attracted all these eager crowds by numberless benefits, so that she might out of all make for her Son a kingdom. Already, dearly-beloved sons, you have been led by this gentle mother; already you have gone straight to her, placing yourselves under her protection; and already of your

own accord you devote to her yourselves, all that
you have, and your country. It is truly a spectacle
worthy of men and of angels to see these eager
legions of Christian men and women, who, without
any instigation from ecclesiastical authority, but only
to its great joy and under its moderating influence,
pour themselves spontaneously into the sanctuaries
to ask pardon for having so long kept aloof from
God, and to offer that humble and contrite heart
which knows no repulse. When we consider that
all these evils originated with those who at the end
of the last century seized the supreme power, intro-
ducing the horrors of a new right, and propagating
the fictions of an insensate doctrine; when we remember that from that source, too, came the perverse
use of the forces and the armies from whence, amid
the total subversion of political power in Europe,
came those seeds of disorder which, each day being
scattered further and further, have little by little
conducted the world to the condition of ceaseless
disturbance—we feel an extreme joy at seeing the
return of France to God beginning with *éclat*, and
begun by those who have been deputed to busy
themselves with public affairs, to make the laws and
govern the people, and by those who, placed at the
head of the land and sea forces, reform the force of
the nation. This concord of right and of might to
render homage to the Most High, to whom belongs
all strength and wisdom, presages a future in which
the reign of error will be destroyed, and in which,

consequently, the origin of evils will be destroyed to the very root. It gives, at the same time, the hope of a perfect reorganisation of things, of a solid tranquillity, and a full restoration of the greatness and glory of France. For He who is great by power, by judgment, and by justice will give wisdom, intelligence, and firmness to those who believe in Him with a perfect heart, and He will scatter with munificence His gifts of grace among the people who devote themselves to Him, and who trust in Him. This is what we augur for you; this is what we augur for your country, dearly-beloved sons. In this hope, as pledge of the support of heaven, and as witness of our paternal affection, we give with our whole heart, to you and the whole of France, our Apostolic Benediction.

Given at Rome, near St. Peter's, the 24th July 1873, in the 28th year of our Pontificate.

Pius IX., *Pope.*

ORDER OF DEVOTIONS.

1. MONDAY, Sept. 1, at 7 P.M., in the Pro-Cathedral, Kensington :
(a) Compline.
(b) Sermon, followed by the Hymn of the Sacred Heart.
(c) Benediction of the Blessed Sacrament.

2. TUESDAY, Sept. 2.

(a) Holy Mass in Warwick-street and other churches, at 6 A.M.
(b) As soon as the train starts, the *Itinerarium*, followed by the *Litany of the Sacred Heart*, should be said in each compartment. Seven Paters and Aves for the Pope, the persecuted Bishops, and the Church.
(c) Between London and Newhaven, the Joyful Mysteries of the Rosary to be said publicly for the conversion of bad Catholics.
(d) In the port of Dieppe, before landing, the *Magnificat* will be sung.
(e) Between Dieppe and Rouen, the Sorrowful Mysteries of the Rosary, followed by prayers

for the conversion of England, to be said in
common.

(*f*) An hour's silence after leaving Rouen, to allow
time for the Divine Office and private devotions.

(*g*) The Glorious Mysteries of the Rosary to be said
in common, shortly before reaching Paris,
for the conversion of sinners.

(*h*) In Paris, about 8 P.M., in the Church of the
Jesuit Fathers, Rue de Sèvres, Sermon, followed by Benediction of the Blessed Sacrament.

WEDNESDAY, Sept. 3.

(*a*) Holy Mass at 5.30, in Notre Dame des Victoires.

(*b*) On the journey from Paris to Paray the same
prayers will be said, the same order and
about the same time will be followed, as
yesterday.

(*c*) Arriving at Paray, the Procession will be formed
and walk to the shrine singing : 1. 'Jesus,
my Lord, my God, my all ;' 2. The 'Ave
Maris Stella ;' 3. 'Immaculate ;' 4. 'To
Jesu's Heart, all burning.'

(*d*) In the Church of the Saint's Shrine, if time
will allow, Benediction of the Blessed
Sacrament, followed by the Hymn, 'God
bless our Pope.'

(*e*) Confessions will be heard afterwards in the
parish church.

4. THURSDAY, Sept. 4.

(*a*) From midnight, the Altar of the Apparition will be reserved for the Priests of the Pilgrimage.

(*b*) The Mass of the General Communion will be at 8. After the Gospel there will be an instruction, followed by the Act of Reparation for our own sins and those of our nation.

(*c*) At 3 P.M., Solemn Vespers of our Lady, followed by an instruction preparatory to the Act of Consecration of our Nation to the Sacred ˙Heart. The Benediction of the Blessed Sacrament and *Te Deum* will close the Public Devotions of the Pilgrimage.

N.B. At the end of each exercise the following should be repeated :

Cor Jesu sacratissimum, miserere nobis !
Cor Mariæ immaculatum, ora pro nobis !
Beata Margarita Maria, ora pro nobis !

FORM OF CONSECRATION TO THE SACRED HEART.

O MOST sweet Jesus, fountain of charity, Father of Mercies, and God of all consolation, who hast deigned to lay open to us, miserable and unworthy sinners, the unspeakable riches of thy Heart, we give thee thanks for all the blessings and benefits vouchsafed to men, and especially to the Priests and people of our country: above all, we thank thee for the institution of the Blessed Sacrament, in which thou abidest with us, a living and continual sacrifice.

Farther, in reparation for the injuries and insults offered by ourselves and by others to thy most loving Heart in this Adorable Sacrament, we hereby consecrate ourselves to thy Sacred Heart, with all that we have and all that we are, promising, as far as in us lies, to propagate this devotion to thy Divine Heart.

And now, O Lord, hear the prayer of thy servants. Behold how hell is being filled with souls redeemed by thy Blood. Have compassion, we beseech thee, O most pitiful and loving Saviour, upon the souls in our land, which is solemnly consecrated to thy Heart. Bring home upon thy shoulders to the fold the wanderers in the paths of ignorance and error: touch with the fire of thy charity the hearts that have grown cold and indifferent to thy service. Grant, we implore thee, to our fervent supplications, through the tears and sorrows of thy Heart, through thy Precious Blood and thy bitter Passion and Death, the conversion of innumerable souls, with whom we may praise thee for ever and ever.

Moreover, we choose the ever-blessed Virgin Mary for our Mother; to her most pure heart we also consecrate ourselves, promising our earnest endeavours to spread around us a devo-

tion to this most tender and Immaculate Mother, according to
the mind of the Church.

Lastly, we choose St. Joseph, the foster-father of Jesus, the
spouse of Mary, and the faithful guardian of them both, to be
our patron and protector in life and in death. May he teach
us how to pray, how to live with Jesus and Mary, and how to
die in their arms !

We beseech thee, O Lord Jesus Christ, of thy immense
goodness and clemency, that thou wouldst deign to receive this
oblation of ourselves in the odour of sweetness; and that as
thou hast inspired us with the desire and the will to make it,
so thou wouldst grant us the graces necessary to complete it.
Amen.

PRAYERS FOR THE HOLY FATHER.

Divine and most loving Heart of Jesus Christ, whence the
Church drew her life, behold here before thee thy humble and
trustful children, who with all the earnestness of their hearts
pour out their prayers for our august Head, their Father the
Sovereign Pontiff.

Console him, we beseech thee, O Lord, with thy heavenly
sweetness; strengthen him by thy power, and defend him, that
so he may obtain a complete victory over his enemies, the enemies alike of justice and truth.

Our Father. Hail Mary. Glory.

O Immaculate Virgin Mary, Mother of God, listen to the
prayers which in all humility and confidence we offer to thee
for the Sovereign Pontiff, the Vicar of Jesus Christ : O, by that
resplendent crown of glory with which he adorned thy brow,
in the dogmatic definition of thy Immaculate Conception, console him under the sadness occasioned by the ingratitude of his
children ; support him in the day of grief and of trial ; and obtain for him from thy Only-begotten Son, that even on earth
he may behold in joy the triumph of the Church.

Queen conceived without original sin, pray for us.

Hail Mary, thrice.

B

Blessed Michael, the Archangel, invincible leader of the heavenly host, and thou, St. Joseph, the most pure Spouse of the Virgin Mary; and you also, glorious princes of the earth, the Holy Apostles SS. Peter and Paul; intercede for us with God, that for his own glory, for the glory of the Church, and for the consolation of the faithful throughout the world, he would be pleased again to send his angel from heaven, to rescue the Vicar of Jesus Christ from the hands of his enemies, that he may be entirely free in the exercise of his supreme and infallible teaching authority.

Our Father. Hail Mary. Glory.

That thou wouldst vouchsafe to humble the enemies of Holy Church. We beseech thee, hear us.

Our Father. Hail Mary. Glory.

That thou wouldst vouchsafe to govern and preserve thy Holy Church. We beseech thee, hear us.

Our Father. Hail Mary. Glory.

That thou wouldst vouchsafe to preserve our Apostolic Prelate, and all orders of the Church, in holy religion. We beseech thee, hear us.

Our Father. Hail Mary. Glory.

V. Let us pray for our Sovereign Pontiff Pius.

R. The Lord preserve him and give him life, and make him blessed upon the earth, and deliver him not into the hands of his enemies.

Let us pray.

Almighty, everlasting God, have mercy on thy servant Pius, our Sovereign Pontiff, and direct him, according to thy clemency, into the way of everlasting salvation, that, by thy grace, he may both desire those things that are pleasing to thee, and perform them with all his strength.

His Holiness has granted, Nov. 29th, 1870, 100 days' indulgence daily to all the faithful who, with contrition, shall recite the above prayers for the Holy Father.

PRAISES OF THE HOLY NAME OF GOD.

To be said after Mass and Benediction.

Blessed be God.

Blessed be his holy name.

Blessed be Jesus Christ, true God and true Man.

Blessed be the name of Jesus.

Blessed be Jesus in the Most Holy Sacrament of the Altar.

Blessed be the great Mother of God, Mary most holy.

Blessed be her Holy and Immaculate Conception.

Blessed be the name of Mary, Virgin and Mother.

Blessed be God in his Angels and in his Saints.

To all who should devoutly and with a contrite heart recite the above Act of Praise, Pope Pius VII., by a Rescript of July 23d, 1801, granted an indulgence of one year; and our Holy Father, Pope Pius IX., by a decree of the Sacred Congregation of Indulgences, dated August 8th, 1847, has granted a Plenary Indulgence once a month to all those who at least once a day recite the said Act, provided that, being truly contrite, they confess and communicate, and visit some church or public oratory, and pray there according to the intention of his Holiness.

————

AN ACT OF REPARATION TO THE SACRED HEART OF JESUS.

O adorable Heart of my God and Saviour, filled with a lively sorrow at the thought of the injuries which thou hast received, and art every day receiving, in the august Sacrament of the altar, I prostrate myself at thy feet, to make thee an act of humble reparation for all that thou hast suffered. O that by my reverence, by my devotion, I could make amends to thy outraged majesty! O that I could do so, even at the sacrifice of my life! Call to mind thy mercies, O Jesus, and grant me the pardon which I beg for so many impious, heretical, and slothful Christians, who dishonour thee, and above all for myself, who have so often offended thee. Remember not my ingratitude; but remember that thy divine Heart, bearing the

burden of my sins, was afflicted even unto death. Let not thy
sufferings and thy blood be in vain; destroy in me my sinful
heart, and give me one according to thine own—a humble and
a contrite heart; a heart that is pure and full of horror for
sin; a heart that henceforth may be as a victim wholly consecrated to thy glory, and inflamed with the sacred fire of thy
love. And for my part, I promise thee, O most sweet Jesus,
to endeavour for the future, as much as in me lies, by my devotion in church, by my diligence in visiting thee in the Sacrament of the altar, by my fervour in receiving thee in the holy
Communion, to make reparation for the irreverences, the pro-
fanations, and the sacrileges which I deplore in the bitterness
of my soul. Amen.

_____

LITANY OF THE SACRED HEART OF JESUS.

Lord, have mercy.
Lord, have mercy.
Christ, have mercy.
Christ, have mercy.
Lord, have mercy.
Lord, have mercy.
Christ, hear us.
Christ, graciously hear us.
God the Father of heaven,
God the Son, Redeemer of the world,
God the Holy Ghost,
Holy Trinity, one God,
Heart of Jesus,
Heart of Jesus, hypostati-cally united with the Word of God,
Heart of Jesus, Sanctuary of the Divinity,
Heart of Jesus, Temple of the Holy Trinity,
Heart of Jesus, Abyss of wisdom,

Have mercy on us.

Heart of Jesus, Ocean of goodness,
Heart of Jesus, Throne of mercy,
Heart of Jesus, Treasure inexhaustible,
Heart of Jesus, of whose fulness we have all re-ceived,
Heart of Jesus, our Peace and our Atonement,
Heart of Jesus, Model of all virtues,
Heart of Jesus, infinitely loving, and infinitely wor-thy of love,
Heart of Jesus, Fountain of water springing up into everlasting life,
Heart of Jesus, in which the Father is well pleased,
Heart of Jesus, the Pro-pitiation for our sins,

Have mercy on us.

Heart of Jesus, filled with bitterness for our sakes,

Heart of Jesus, sorrowful in the Garden even unto death,

Heart of Jesus, saturated with revilings,

Heart of Jesus, wounded with love,

Heart of Jesus, pierced with a lance,

Heart of Jesus, exhausted of thy blood upon the Cross,

Heart of Jesus, bruised for our sins,

Heart of Jesus, still outraged by ungrateful men in the most holy Sacrament of love,

Heart of Jesus, Refuge of sinners,

Heart of Jesus, Strength of the weak,

Heart of Jesus, Comfort of the afflicted,

Heart of Jesus, Perseverance of the just,

Heart of Jesus, Salvation of them that hope in thee,

Heart of Jesus, Hope of them that die in thee,

Heart of Jesus, sweet Support of those who worship thee,

Heart of Jesus, our Helper in our many and great tribulations,

Heart of Jesus, Delight of all the Saints,

Have mercy on us.

Lamb of God, who takest away the sins of the world,

Spare us, O Lord.

Lamb of God, who takest away the sins of the world,

Graciously hear us, O Lord.

Lamb of God, who takest away the sins of the world,

Have mercy on us.

Christ, hear us.

Christ, graciously hear us.

V. Jesus, who art meek and humble of heart,

R. Make our heart like unto thy Heart.

Let us pray.

Grant, we beseech thee, Almighty God, that, as in worshipping the most sacred Heart of thy well-beloved Son, we call to mind the special benefits which his love hath bestowed upon us, so we may ever enjoy the fruits which flow therefrom. Through the same Christ our Lord. Amen.

ITINERARY.

Ant. In the way of peace.

The Benedictus, or Canticle of Zachary.

Benedictus Dominus Deus Israel : quia visitavit, et fecit redemptionem plebis suæ.

Et erexit cornu salutis nobis : in domo David pueri sui.

Sicut locutus est per os sanctorum : qui a sæculo sunt, prophetarum ejus.

Salutem ex inimicis nostris : et de manu omnium qui oderunt nos.

Ad faciendam misericordiam cum patribus nostris : et memorari testamenti sui sancti.

Jusjurandum quod juravit ad Abraham patrem nostrum : daturum se nobis :

Ut sine timore, de manu inimicorum nostrorum liberati : serviamus illi,

In sanctitate et justitia coram ipso : omnibus diebus nostris.

. Et tu, puer, propheta Altissimi vocaberis : præibis enim ante faciem Domini parare vias ejus.

Ad dandam scientiam salutis plebi ejus : in remissionem peccatorum eorum.

1 Blessed be the Lord God of Israel : for he hath visited, and wrought the redemption of his people.

2 And hath raised up a horn of salvation to us : in the house of his servant David.

3 As he spake by the mouth of his holy prophets : who are from the beginning.

4 Salvation from our enemies : and from the hand of all that hate us.

5 To perform mercy to our fathers : and to remember his holy testament.

6 The oath that he sware to Abraham our father : that he would grant unto us :

7 That being delivered from the hands of our enemies : we may serve him without fear,

8 In holiness and justice before him : all the days of our life.

9 And thou, child, shalt be called the prophet of the Highest : for thou shalt go before the face of the Lord to prepare his ways.

10 To give knowledge of salvation unto his people : for the remission of their sins.

Per viscera misericordiæ Dei nostri : in quibus visitavit nos oriens ex alto.

Illuminare his qui in tenebris et in umbra mortis sedent : ad dirigendos pedes nostros in viam pacis.

Gloria Patri.

11 Through the bowels of the mercy of our God : whereby the orient from on high hath visited us.

12 To enlighten them that sit in darkness, and in the shadow of death : to direct our feet into the way of peace.

Glory be to the Father.

Ant. In the way of peace and prosperity may the Lord, the almighty and merciful, direct our steps. And may the angel Raphael accompany us on the way, that we may return to our home in peace, safety, and joy.

Lord, have mercy.

Christ, have mercy.

Lord, have mercy.

Our Father, *secretly.*

V. And lead us not into temptation.

R. But deliver us from evil.

V. Save thy servants.

R. Who trust in thee, O my God.

V. Send us help, O Lord, from thy holy place.

R. And defend us out of Sion.

V. Be unto us, O Lord, a tower of strength.

R. From the face of the enemy.

V. Let not the enemy prevail against us.

R. Nor the son of iniquity approach to hurt us.

V. Blessed be the Lord from day to day.

R. May the God of our salvation make our way prosperous before us.

V. Show us thy way, O Lord,

R. And teach us thy paths.

V. O, that our ways were directed.

R. To keep thy righteous laws.

V. The crooked ways shall be made straight.

R. And the rough places smooth.

V. God hath given his angels charge concerning thee.

R. To keep thee in all thy ways.

V. Lord, hear my prayer.

R. And let my cry come unto thee.

O God, who madest the sons of Israel to walk with dry feet through the midst of the sea, and who didst open to the three magi, by the guiding of a star, the way that led to thee; grant to us, we beseech thee, a prosperous journey and a time of tranquillity, that, attended by thy holy angel, we may happily arrive at that place whither we are journeying, and finally at the haven of eternal salvation.

O God, who broughtest Abraham thy son out of the land of the Chaldees, and didst preserve him unhurt through all his journeyings, we beseech thee vouchsafe to keep us thy servants; be unto us our support in our setting out, our solace on the way, our shadow in the heat, our covering in the rain and cold, the chariot of our weariness, the fortress of our adversity, our staff in the ways of slipperiness, and our harbour in shipwreck, that under thy guidance we may reach in prosperity the object of our journey, and at length return to our home in safety.

Give ear, O Lord, we beseech thee, to our supplications, and dispose the way of thy servants in the blessedness of thy salvation, that amidst all the various changes of this our life and pilgrimage we may ever be protected by thy help.

Vouchsafe to thy people, we beseech thee, Almighty God, that they may walk onward in the way of salvation, and, by following the exhortations of the blessed forerunner John, may come safe to the presence of him whom he preached, Jesus Christ thy Son, our Lord, who liveth and reigneth with thee, in the unity of the Holy Spirit, God for ever and ever. Amen.

V. Let us proceed in peace.

R. In the name of the Lord.   Amen.

EXPOSITION AND BENEDICTION OF THE MOST HOLY SACRAMENT.

When the Priest opens the Tabernacle, and incenses the Blessed Sacrament, is sung the Hymn,

O salutaris Hostia,	O saving Victim, opening wide
Quæ cœli pandis ostium:	The gate of heav'n to man below!
Bella premunt hostilia,	Our foes press on from every side;
Da robur, fer auxilium.	Thine aid supply, thy strength bestow.
Uni trinoque Domino	To thy great name be endless praise,
Sit sempiterna gloria,	Immortal Godhead, one in three!
Qui vitam sine termino	O, grant us endless length of days
Nobis donet in patria.	In our true native land with thee.
Amen.	Amen.

LITANY OF THE BLESSED VIRGIN,
COMMONLY CALLED THE LITANY OF LORETTO.

Sub tuum præsidium confugimus, sancta Dei Genitrix, nostras deprecationes ne despicias in necessitatibus nostris; sed a periculis cunctis libera nos semper, Virgo gloriosa et benedicta.

We fly to thy patronage, O holy Mother of God, despise not our petitions in our necessities; but deliver us always from all dangers, O glorious and blessed Virgin.

Kyrie eleison. — Lord, have mercy.
Kyrie eleison. — *Lord, have mercy.*
Christe eleison. — Christ, have mercy.
Christe eleison. — *Christ, have mercy.*
Kyrie eleison. — Lord, have mercy.
Kyrie eleison. — *Lord, have mercy.*
Christe audi nos. — Christ, hear us.
Christe exaudi nos. — *Christ, graciously hear us.*

Pater de cœlis Deus,	God the Father of heaven,	*Have mercy, &c.*
Fili Redemptor mundi Deus,	God the Son, Redeemer of the world,	
Spiritus Sancte Deus,	God the Holy Ghost,	
Sancta Trinitas, unus Deus,	Holy Trinity, one God,	
Sancta Maria,	Holy Mary,	
Sancta Dei Genitrix,	Holy Mother of God,	
Sancta Virgo virginum,	Holy Virgin of virgins,	
Mater Christi,	Mother of Christ,	
Mater divinæ gratiæ,	Mother of divine grace,	
Mater purissima,	Mother most pure,	
Mater castissima,	Mother most chaste,	
Mater inviolata,	Mother inviolate,	
Mater intemerata,	Mother undefiled,	
Mater amabilis,	Mother most amiable,	
Mater admirabilis,	Mother most admirable,	
Mater Creatoris,	Mother of our Creator,	
Mater Salvatoris,	Mother of our Saviour,	
Virgo prudentissima,	Virgin most prudent,	*Pray for us.*
Virgo veneranda,	Virgin most venerable,	
Virgo prædicanda,	Virgin most renowned,	
Virgo potens,	Virgin most powerful,	
Virgo clemens,	Virgin most merciful,	
Virgo fidelis,	Virgin most faithful,	
Speculum justitiæ,	Mirror of justice,	
Sedes sapientiæ,	Seat of wisdom,	
Causa nostræ lætitiæ;	Cause of our joy,	
Vas spirituale,	Spiritual Vessel,	
Vas honorabile,	Vessel of honour,	
Vas insigne devotionis,	Vessel of singular devotion,	
Rosa mystica,	Mystical Rose,	
Turris Davidica,	Tower of David,	
Turris eburnea,	Tower of ivory,	
Domus aurea,	House of gold,	
Fœderis arca,	Ark of the covenant,	
Janua cœli,	Gate of heaven,	
Stella matutina,	Morning star,	
Salus infirmorum,	Health of the sick,	
Refugium peccatorum,	Refuge of sinners,	

Miserere nobis.

Ora pro nobis.

Consolatrix afflictorum,

Auxilium Christianorum,

Regina Angelorum,

Regina Patriarcharum,

Regina Prophetarum,

Regina Apostolorum,

Regina Martyrum,

Regina Confessorum,

Regina Virginum,

Regina Sanctorum omnium,

Regina sine labe originali concepta,

Agnus Dei, qui tollis peccata mundi,

Parce nobis, Domine.

Agnus Dei, qui tollis peccata mundi,

Exaudi nos, Domine.

Agnus Dei, qui tollis peccata mundi,

Miserere nobis.

Christe audi nos.

Christe exaudi nos.

Ant. Sub tuum præsidium confugimus, sancta Dei Genitrix, nostras deprecationes ne despicias in necessitatibus nostris; sed a periculis cunctis libera nos semper, Virgo gloriosa et benedicta.

. *V.* Ora pro nobis, sancta Dei Genitrix.

R. Ut digni efficiamur promissionibus Christi.

Oremus.

Gratiam tuam, quæsumus, Domine, mentibus nostris in-

Ora pro nobis.

Comforter of the afflicted,

Help of Christians,

Queen of Angels,

Queen of Patriarchs,

Queen of Prophets,

Queen of Apostles,

Queen of Martyrs,

Queen of Confessors,

Queen of Virgins,

Queen of all Saints,

Queen conceived without original sin,

Lamb of God, who takest away the sins of the world,

Spare us, O Lord.

Lamb of God, who takest away the sins of the world,

Graciously hear us, O Lord.

Lamb of God, who takest away the sins of the world,

Have mercy on us.

Christ, hear us.

Christ, graciously hear us.

Ant. We fly to thy patronage, O holy Mother of God, despise not our petitions in our necessities; but deliver us always from all dangers, O glorious and blessed Virgin.

V. Pray for us, O holy Mother of God.

R. That we may be made worthy of the promises of Christ.

Let us pray.

Pour forth, we beseech thee, O Lord, thy grace into our

Pray for us.

funde : ut qui, Angelo nun-tiante, Christi Filii tui Incar-nationem cognovimus, per Pas-sionem + ejus et Crucem ad Resurrectionis gloriam perdu-camur. Per eundem Christum Dominum nostrum. Amen.

hearts; that we, to whom the Incarnation of Christ thy Son was made known by the mes-sage of an Angel, may, by his Passion + and Cross, be brought to the glory of his Resurrection. Through, &c. Amen.

Tantum ergo Sacramentum
Veneremur cernui :
Et antiquum documentum

Down in adoration falling,
Lo! the sacred Host we hail;
Lo! o'er ancient forms depart-ing,

Novo cedat ritui ;
Præstet fides supplementum
Sensuum defectui.

Newer rites of grace prevail;
Faith for all defects supplying
Where the feeble senses fail.

Genitori, Genitoque
Laus et jubilatio,

To the everlasting Father,
And the Son who reigns on high,

Salus, honor, virtus quoque

With the Holy Ghost proceed-ing

Sit et benedictio :
Procedenti ab utroque
Compar sit laudatio.

Forth from each eternally,
Be salvation, honour, blessing,
Might, and endless majesty !

Then are sung the following Versicle and Prayer.

V. Panem de cœlo præsti-tisti eis.

R. Omne delectamentum in se habentum.

Deus, qui nobis sub Sacra-mento mirabili, passionis tuæ memoriam reliquisti: tribue, quæsumus, ita nos corporis et sanguinis tui sacra mysteria venerari; ut redemptionis tuæ fructum in nobis jugiter sen-tiamus. Qui vivis, &c. Amen.

V. Thou didst give them bread from heaven.

R. Containing in itself all sweetness.

O God, who, under a won-derful Sacrament, hast left us a memorial of thy passion; grant us, we beseech thee, so to venerate the sacred mys-teries of thy body and blood, that we may ever feel within us the fruit of thy redemption. Who livest, &c. Amen.

VESPERS.

✝ O divine and adorable Lord Jesus Christ, who hast graciously redeemed us by thy bitter passion and death, we offer up these Vespers to thy honour and glory, humbly beseeching thee, through thy dolorous agony and bloody sweat which thou didst suffer in the garden, to grant us true contrition of heart, and sorrow for our sins, with a pious resolution never more to offend thee, but to satisfy thy divine justice for our past iniquities. Amen.

Ave Maria (*secreto*).

V. Deus, in adjutorium meum intende.

R. Domine, ad adjuvandum me festina.

Gloria Patri.

Hail Mary (*secretly*).

V. O God, come to my assistance.

R. O Lord, make haste to help me.

Glory be to the Father.

OFFICE 1.

Ant. Dum esset rex.

Ant. While the king.

Psalm cix. *Dixit Dominus.*

Dixit Dominus Domino meo: Sede a dextris meis:

Donec ponam inimicos tuos: scabellum pedum tuorum.

Virgam virtutis tuæ emittet Dominus ex Sion: dominare in medio inimicorum tuorum.

Tecum principium in die virtutis tuæ in splendoribus Sanctorum: ex utero ante luciferum genui te.

Juravit Dominus, et non pœnitebit eum: Tu es sacerdos in æternum secundum ordinem Melchisedec.

1 The Lord said to my Lord: Sit thou at my right hand:

2 Until I make thine enemies: thy footstool.

3 The Lord shall send forth the rod of thy power from out of Sion: rule thou in the midst of thine enemies.

4 Thine shall be the dominion in the day of thy power, amid the brightness of the Saints: from the womb, before the day-star, have I begotten thee.

5 The Lord hath sworn, and will not repent: Thou art a priest for ever according to the order of Melchisedec.

Dominus a dextris tuis : confregit in die iræ suæ reges.

6 The Lord upon thy right hand : hath overthrown kings in the day of his wrath.

Judicabit in nationibus, implebit ruinas : conquassabit capita in terra multorum.

7 He shall judge among the nations, he shall fulfil destructions : he shall smite in sunder the heads in the land of many.

De torrente in via bibet, propterea exaltabit caput.

8 He shall drink of the brook in the way : therefore shall he lift up his head.

Gloria Patri.

Glory be to the Father.

OFFICE 1.

Ant. Dum esset rex in accubitu suo, nardus mea dedit odorem suavitatis.

Ant. While the king was reposing, my spikenard yielded the odour of sweetness.

Ant. Læva ejus.

Ant. His left hand.

Psalm cxii. *Laudate, pueri.*

Laudate, pueri, Dominum : laudate nomen Domini.

1 Praise the Lord, ye children : praise ye the name of the Lord.

Sit nomen Domini benedictum : ex hoc nunc, et usque in sæculum.

2 Blessed be the name of the Lord : from this time forth, for evermore.

A solis ortu usque ad occasum : laudabile nomen Domini.

3 From the rising up of the sun unto the going down of the same : the name of the Lord is worthy to be praised.

Excelsus super omnes gentes Dominus : et super cœlos gloria ejus.

4 The Lord is high above all nations : and his glory above the heavens.

Quis sicut Dominus Deus noster, qui in altis habitat : et humilia respicit in cœlo et in terra ?

5 Who is like unto the Lord our God, who dwelleth on high : and regardeth the things that are lowly in heaven and in earth ?

Suscitans a terra inopem : et de stercore erigens pauperem :

6 Who raiseth up the needy from the earth : and lifteth the poor from off the dunghill :

Ut collocet eum cum principibus : cum principibus populi sui.

Qui habitare facit sterilem in domo : matrem filiorum lætantem.

Gloria Patria.

7 That he may set him with the princes : even with the princes of his people.

8 Who maketh the barren woman to dwell in her house : the joyful mother of children.

Glory be to the Father.

OFFICE 1.

Ant. Læva ejus sub capite meo, et dextera illius amplexabitur me.

Ant. Nigra sum.

Ant. His left hand under my head, and his right hand shall embrace me.

Ant. I am black.

Psalm cxxi. *Lætatus sum in his.*

Lætatus sum in his quæ dicta sunt mihi : In domum Domini ibimus.

Stantes erant pedes nostri : in atriis tuis, Jerusalem.

Jerusalem, quæ ædificatur ut civitas : cujus participatio ejus in idipsum.

Illuc enim ascenderunt tribus, tribus Domini : testimonium Israel, ad confitendum nomini Domini.

Quia illic sederunt sedes in judicio : sedes super domum David.

Rogate quæ ad pacem sunt, Jerusalem : et abundantia diligentibus te.

Fiat pax in virtute tua : et abundantia in turribus tuis.

1 I was glad at the things that were said unto me : We will go into the house of the Lord.

2 Our feet were wont to stand : in thy courts, O Jerusalem.

3 Jerusalem, which is built as a city : that is at unity with itself.

4 For thither did the tribes go up, the tribes of the Lord : the testimony of Israel, to praise the name of the Lord.

5 For there are set the seats of judgment : the seats over the house of David.

6 Pray ye for the things that are for the peace of Jerusalem : and plenteousness be to them that love thee.

7 Let peace be in thy strength : and plenteousness in thy towers.

Propter fratres meos et proximos meos : loquebar pacem de te.

Propter domum Domini Dei nostri : quæsivi bona tibi.

Gloria Patri.

8 For my brethren and companions' sake : I spake peace concerning thee.

9 Because of the house of the Lord our God : I have sought good things for thee.

Glory be to the Father.

OFFICE 1.

Ant. Nigra sum, sed formosa, filiæ Jerusalem : ideo dilexit me rex, et introduxit me in cubiculum suum.

Ant. Jam hiems transiit.

Ant. I am black, but beautiful, O daughters of Jerusalem : therefore hath the king loved me, and brought me into his chamber.

Ant. Now is the winter past.

Psalm cxxvi. *Nisi Dominus.*

Nisi Dominus ædificaverit domum : in vanum laboraverunt qui ædificant eam.

Nisi Dominus custodierit civitatem : frustra vigilat qui custodit eam.

Vanum est vobis ante lucem surgere : surgite postquam sederitis, qui manducatis panem doloris.

Cum dederit dilectis suis somnum : ecce hæreditas Domini filii, merces fructus ventris.

Sicut sagittæ in manu potentis : ita filii excussorum.

Beatus vir qui implevit desiderium suum ex ipsis : non

1 Unless the Lord build the house : they labour in vain that build it.

2 Unless the Lord keep the city : he watcheth in vain that keepeth it.

3 In vain ye rise before the light : rise not till ye have rested, O ye that eat the bread of sorrow.

4 When he hath given sleep to his beloved : lo, children are an heritage from the Lord, and the fruit of the womb a reward.

5 Like as arrows in the hand of the mighty one : so are the children of those who have been cast out.

6 Blessed is the man whose desire is satisfied with them :

confundetur, cum loquetur inimicis suis in porta.

Gloria Patri.

he shall not be confounded, when he speaketh with his enemies in the gate.

Glory be to the Father.

Psalm cxlvii. *Lauda Jerusalem.*

Lauda Jerusalem Dominum: lauda Deum tuum, Sion.

Quoniam confortavit seras portarum tuarum : benedixit filiis tuis in te.

Qui posuit fines tuos pacem : et adipe frumenti satiat te.

Qui emittit eloquium suum terræ : velociter currit sermo ejus.

Qui dat nivem sicut lanam : nebulam sicut cineram spargit.

Mittit crystallum suum sicut buccellas : ante faciem frigoris ejus quis sustinebit?

Emittet verbum suum, et liquefaciet ea : flabit spiritus ejus, et fluent aquæ.

Qui annuntiat verbum suum Jacob : justitias et judicia sua Israel.

Non fecit taliter omni nationi : et judicia sua non manifestavit eis.

Gloria Patri.

1 Praise the Lord, O Jerusalem : praise thy God, O Sion.

2 For he hath strengthened the bars of thy gates : he hath blessed thy children within thee.

3 He hath made peace within thy borders : and filleth thee with the fatness of corn.

4 He sendeth forth his commandment on the earth : his word runneth very swiftly.

5 He giveth snow like wool : he scattereth the hoar-frost like ashes.

6 He sendeth his ice like morsels : who is able to abide his frost?

7 He shall send forth his word, and melt them : he shall blow with his wind, and the waters shall flow.

8 He maketh known his word unto Jacob : his statutes and ordinances unto Israel.

9 He hath not dealt so with any nation : neither hath he showed them his judgments.

Glory be to the Father.

c

OFFICE 1.

Ant. Speciosa facta es et suavis in deliciis tuis, sancta Dei Genitrix.

Ant. Thou art become beautiful and sweet in thy delights, O holy Mother of God.

THE LITTLE CHAPTER.

Office 1 *and* 3.   Ecclus. xxiv. 14.

Ab initio et ante sæcula creata sum, et usque ad futurum sæculum non desinam, et in habitatione sancta coram ipso ministravi.

From the beginning, and before the world was I created, and unto the world to come I shall not cease to be, and in the holy dwelling-place I have ministered before him.

R. Deo gratias.

R. Thanks be to God.

Ave, maris stella,
Dei Mater alma,
Atque semper Virgo,
Felix cœli porta.

Hail, thou Star of ocean !
    Portal of the sky !
Ever Virgin Mother
    Of the Lord most high !

Sumens illud Ave
Gabrielis ore,
Funda nos in pace,
Mutans Evæ nomen.

O, by Gabriel's Ave,
    Utter'd long ago,
Eva's name reversing,
    'Stablish peace below.

Solve vincla reis,
Profer lumen cæcis,
Mala nostra pelle,
Bona cuncta posce.

Break the captive's fetters ;
    Light on blindness pour ;
All our ills expelling,
    Every bliss implore.

Monstra te esse Matrem
Sumat per te preces
Qui pro nobis natus,
Tulit esse tuus.

Show thyself a Mother ;
    Offer him our sighs,
Who for us Incarnate
    Did not thee despise.

Virgo singularis,
Inter omnes mitis,
Nos culpis solutos
Mites fac et castos.

Virgin of all virgins,
    To thy shelter take us !
Gentlest of the gentle,
    Chaste and gentle make us !

Vitam præsta puram,
Iter para tutum ;
Ut videntes Jesum
Semper collætemur.

Sit laus Deo Patri,
Summum Christo decus,
Spiritui Sancto,
Tribus honor unus. Amen.

V. Diffusa est gratia in labiis tuis.
R. Propterea benedixit te Deus in æternum.

Still, as on we journey,
Help our weak endeavour;
Till with thee and Jesus
We rejoice for ever.

Through the highest heaven,
To the Almighty Three,
Father, Son, and Spirit,
One same glory be. Amen.

V. Grace is poured abroad on thy lips.
R. Therefore hath the Lord blessed thee for ever.

OFFICE 1.

Ant. Beata Mater.

Ant. Blessed Mother.

The Magnificat.

Magnificat : anima mea Dominum.

Et exultavit spiritus meus : in Deo salutari meo.

Quia respexit humilitatem ancillæ suæ : ecce enim ex hoc beatam me dicent omnes generationes.

Quia fecit mihi magna qui potens est : et sanctum nomen ejus.

Et misericordia ejus a progenie in progenies : timentibus eum.

Fecit potentiam in brachio suo : dispersit superbos mente cordis sui.

1 My soul doth magnify : the Lord.

2 And my spirit hath rejoiced : in God my Saviour.

3 For he hath regarded the lowliness of his handmaid : for behold from henceforth all generations shall call me blessed.

4 For he that is mighty hath done great things unto me : and holy is his name.

5 And his mercy is from generation to generation : unto them that fear him.

6 He hath showed strength with his arm : he hath scattered the proud in the imagination of their heart.

Deposuit potentes de sede : et exaltavit humiles.

7 He hath put down the mighty from their seat : and hath exalted the humble.

Esurientes implevit bonis : et divites dimisit inanes.

8 He hath filled the hungry with good things : and the rich he hath sent empty away.

Suscepit Israel puerum suum : recordatus misericordiæ suæ.

9 He hath upholden his servant Israel : being mindful of his mercy.

Sicut locutus est ad patres nostros : Abraham, et semini ejus in sæcula.

10 As he spake unto our fathers : to Abraham and his seed for ever.

Gloria Patri.

Glory be to the Father.

OFFICE 1.

Ant. Beata Mater et intacta Virgo, gloriosa Regina mundi, intercede pro nobis ad Dominum.

Ant. Blessed Mother and inviolate Virgin, glorious Queen of the world, intercede for us with the Lord.

V. Domine, exaudi orationem meam.

V. O Lord, hear my prayer.

R. Et clamor meus ad te veniat.

R. And let my cry come unto thee.

Oremus.

Let us pray.

Concede nos famulos tuos, quæsumus, Domine Deus, perpetua mentis et corporis sanitate gaudere ; et gloriosa beatæ Mariæ semper Virginis intercessione, a præsenti liberari tristitia, et æterna perfrui lætitia. Per Dominum nostrum Christum.

Grant, we beseech thee, O Lord God, that we, thy servants, may enjoy perpetual health, both of mind and body; and by the glorious intercession of blessed Mary ever Virgin, may be delivered from present sorrow, and attain unto eternal joy. Through Christ our Lord.

R. Amen.

R. Amen.

The Antiphon.

Salve, Regina, mater misericordiæ;

Vita, dulcedo, et spes nostra, salve.

Ad te clamamus, exules filii Hevæ;

Ad te suspiramus, gementes et flentes in hac lacrymarum valle.

Eia ergo, Advocata nostra,

Illos tuos misericordes oculos ad nos converte;

Et Jesum, benedictum fructum ventris tui,

Nobis post hoc exilium ostende,

O clemens, O pia, O dulcis Virgo Maria.

V. Ora pro nobis, sancta Dei Genitrix.

R. Ut digni efficiamur promissionibus Christi.

Oremus.

Omnipotens sempiterne Deus, qui gloriosæ Virginis Matris Mariæ corpus et animam, ut dignum Filii tui habitaculum effici mereretur, Spiritu Sancto co-operante, præparasti; da, ut cujus commemoratione lætamur, ejus pia inter-

Mother of mercy, hail, O gentle Queen!

Our life, our sweetness, and our hope, all hail!

Children of Eve,

To thee we cry from our sad banishment;

To thee we send our sighs,

Weeping and mourning in this tearful vale.

Come, then, our Advocate;

O, turn on us those pitying eyes of thine:

And our long exile past,

Show us at last

Jesus, of thy pure womb the fruit divine.

O Virgin Mary, mother blest!

O sweetest, gentlest, holiest!

V. Pray for us, O holy Mother of God.

R. That we may be made worthy of the promises of Christ.

Let us pray.

O almighty everlasting God, who, by the coöperation of the Holy Ghost, didst prepare the body and soul of Mary, glorious Virgin and Mother, to become the worthy habitation of thy Son; grant that we may be delivered from instant evils

cessione ab instantibus malis et a morte perpetua liberemur. Per eumdem Christum, &c.

R. Amen.

V. Divinum auxilium maneat semper nobiscum.

and from everlasting death by her pious intercession, in whose commemoration we rejoice. Through the same Christ, &c.

R. Amen.

V. May the divine assistance remain always with us.

———

PRAYERS FOR THE CONVERSION OF ENGLAND.*

Ant. Remember not, O Lord, our offences, nor those of our parents : neither take thou vengeance of our sins.

Then is said one of the following Psalms, with its versicle and prayer, according to the day of the week.

SUNDAY.

From Ps. lxviii. lxx.

Save me, O God, for the waters are come in even unto my soul.

I stick fast in the mire of the deep, and there is no sure standing.

Because for thy sake I have borne reproach ; shame hath covered my face.

I am become a stranger to my brethren, and an alien to the sons of my mother.

For the zeal of thine house hath eaten me up ; and the reproaches of them that reproached thee are fallen upon me.

How great troubles hast thou showed me, many and grievous ; and yet hast thou turned again and refreshed me, and hast brought me back from the depths of the earth.

Thou hast multiplied towards me thy magnificence ; and hast turned again and comforted me.

I will praise the name of

* Composed in Latin for the English College at Rome, in the year 1839, by the Right Rev. Dr. Wiseman.

God with a canticle; and I will magnify him with praise.

For God will save Zion, and the cities of Judah shall be built up.

And they shall dwell there, and acquire it by inheritance.

And the seed of his servants shall possess it: and they that love his name shall dwell therein.

Glory be, &c.

Then is repeated the Ant. Remember not.

Lord, have mercy.
Christ, have mercy.
Lord, have mercy.
Our Father (*in secret*).
V. And lead us not into temptation.
R. But deliver us from evil.
V. Save us, O our God.
R. And gather us from among the nations.
V. That we may give thanks to thy holy name.
R. And may glory in thy praise.
V. Convert us, O Lord God of hosts.
R. And show thy face, and we shall be saved.
V. Convert us, O Lord, and we shall be converted.
R. Renew our days, as from the beginning.
V. O Lord, hear my prayer.
R. And let my cry come unto thee.

Let us pray.

O almighty everlasting God, who hast ordained that men shall be saved by one only true faith; look graciously upon our beloved country, which a deplorable heresy hath too long held captive under the yoke of error; dispel all darkness of ignorance, drive away all vain opinions of false doctrine, and dispose the minds of all to the reasonable obedience of the true faith, that they may return with joy into the bosom of our holy mother the Church. Through Christ our Lord. Amen.

MONDAY.

Ant. Remember not.

From Ps. lxxiii. ci.

O God, why hast thou cast us off unto the end: why is thy wrath enkindled against the sheep of thy pasture?

Remember thy congregation, which thou hast possessed from the beginning.

The sceptre of thine inheritance, which thou hast redeemed; Mount Sion, in which thou hast dwelt.

Thou shalt arise and have mercy upon Sion : for it is time that thou have mercy upon her, yea, the time is come.

For thy servants have delighted in her stones, and they shall have compassion on the earth thereof.

And the Gentiles shall fear thy name, O Lord, and all the kings of the earth thy glory.

For the Lord hath built up Sion, and he shall be seen in his glory.

He hath had regard unto the prayer of the humble, and hath not despised their petition.

Let these things be written for another generation, and the people that shall be created shall praise the Lord.

When the people assemble together, and kings that they may serve the Lord.

The children of thy servants shall continue, and their seed shall be directed for ever.

Glory be, &c.

Ant. Remember not.
Lord, have mercy.
Christ, have mercy.
Lord, have mercy.
Our Father (*in secret*).
V. And lead us not into temptation.
R. But deliver us from evil.
V. The Lord is compassionate and merciful.
R. Long-suffering and plenteous in mercy.
V. He will not always be angry.
R. Neither will he threaten for ever.
V. Convert us, O Lord God of hosts.
R. And show thy face, and we shall be saved.

V. Convert us, O Lord, and we shall be converted.

R. Renew our days, as from the beginning.

V. O Lord, hear my prayer.

R. And let my cry come unto thee.

Let us pray.

Lord God Almighty, who wast pleased to build thy Church upon the foundation of the Apostles, and hast given to their successors alone all authority for the teaching and governing thereof : look graciously upon our beloved country, long since torn from that foundation, and mercifully gather together her people, who are wandering like sheep without shepherds ; that, the multitude of nations flocking to thy holy temple, our hearts may expand with joy and charity. Through Christ our Lord. Amen.

Then are said the prayers at the end.

TUESDAY.

Ant. Remember not.

From Ps. lxxix.

Give ear, O thou that rulest Israel, thou that leadest Joseph like a sheep.

Stir up thy might, and come to save us.

Convert us, O God; and show thy face, and we shall be saved.

O Lord God of hosts, how long wilt thou be angry against the prayer of thy servant ?

Thou hast made us to be a contradiction to our neighbours: and our enemies have scoffed at us:

O God of hosts, convert us ; and show thy face, and we shall be saved.

Thou hast brought a vine out of Egypt ; thou hast cast out the Gentiles, and planted it.

Why hast thou broken down the hedge thereof ; so that all they who pass by the way pluck off the grapes ?

Turn again, O God of hosts; look down from heaven, and see, and visit this vine.

And perfect the same, which thy right hand hath planted.

And we depart not from thee, and we will call upon thy name.

O Lord God of hosts, convert us ; and show thy face, and we shall be saved.

Glory be, &c.

Ant. Remember not.

Lord, have mercy.

Christ, have mercy.

Lord, have mercy.

Our Father (*in secret*).

V. And lead us not into temptation.

R. But deliver us from evil.

V. Await thou the Lord, do manfully.

R. And let thy heart take courage, and wait thou for the Lord.

V. For the Lord will not cast off his people.

R. Neither will he forsake his own inheritance.

V. Convert us, O Lord God of hosts.

R. And show thy face, and we shall be saved.

V. Convert us, O Lord, and we shall be converted.

R. Renew our days, as from the beginning.

V. O Lord, hear my prayer.

R. And let my cry come unto thee.

Let us pray.

O most merciful and gracious God, who, having given to St. Peter the keys of the kingdom of heaven, hast made his Chair the centre of unity and communion, so that whosoever is not within this ark must of necessity suffer shipwreck; look graciously upon our beloved country, in great part separated from this fellowship with the Apostolic See; and grant that, every artifice of the enemy being brought to naught, she may at length, under the guidance of the supreme Pastor whom thou hast mercifully provided for thy flock, find the food of life and the hope of eternal happiness. Who livest and reignest world without end. Amen.

Then are said the prayers at the end.

WEDNESDAY.

Ant. Remember not.

From Ps. lxxxiv.

Thou hast blessed thy land, O Lord; thou hast turned away the captivity of Jacob. Thou hast forgiven the iniquity of thy people; thou hast covered all their sins.

Thou hast softened all thine anger; thou hast turned away from thy wrathful indignation.

Convert thou us, O God our Saviour; and turn away thine anger from us.

Wilt thou be angry with us for ever? or wilt thou stretch out thy wrath from generation to generation?

Thou wilt turn again, O God, and quicken us; and thy people shall rejoice in thee.

Show us, O Lord, thy mercy; and grant us thy salvation.

I will hearken what the Lord God shall say within me; for he will speak peace unto his people;

And unto his saints, and unto them that are converted in heart.

Surely his salvation is nigh unto them that fear him; that glory may dwell in our land.

For the Lord shall put forth his goodness, and our land shall yield her fruit.

Glory be, &c.

Ant. Remember not.
Lord, have mercy.
Christ, have mercy.
Lord, have mercy.
Our Father (*in secret*).
V. And lead us not into temptation.
R. But deliver us from evil.
V. Remember us, O Lord, in thy good will.
R. Visit us in thy salvation.
V. When the Lord shall have turned away the captivity of his people.
R. Jacob shall rejoice, and Israel shall be glad.
V. Convert us, O Lord God of hosts.
R. And show thy face, and we shall be saved.
V. Convert us, O Lord, and we shall be converted.
R. Renew our days, as from the beginning.
V. O Lord, hear my prayer.
R. And let my cry come unto thee.

Let us pray.

O almighty everlasting God, by the counsel of whose goodness the souls of all the faithful are bound together in a communion of prayers and merits, and united in the one only Church of Christ, whether they already reign triumphant in heaven, or, still militant, are straitened in the body, or, sentenced to expiatory sufferings, are being purified from their stains; look graciously upon our beloved country, now too long separated from this communion of saints, and deprived of all the graces which flow therefrom; make her speedily to return into this bond of charity and peace, that, from the opened treasures of thy Church, both living and dead may receive indulgence and pardon. Through Christ our Lord. Amen.

Then are said the prayers at the end.

THURSDAY.

Ant. Remember not.

From Ps. lxxxix.

Lord, thou hast been our refuge, from generation to generation.

Before the mountains were made, or the earth and the world were formed; from eternity and to eternity thou art God.

Turn not man away to be brought low: thou hast said, Be converted, O ye sons of men.

For a thousand years in thy sight are but as yesterday, which is past.

For in thy wrath we have fainted away, and are troubled in thine indignation.

Thou hast set our iniquities before thine eyes; our life in the light of thy countenance.

For all our days are spent; and in thy wrath we have fainted away.

Turn thou again, O Lord, how long? and be entreated in favour of thy servants.

We are filled in the morning with thy mercy; and we have rejoiced and are delighted all our days.

We have rejoiced for the days in which thou hast humbled us; for the years in which we have seen evils.

Look upon thy servants, and upon thy works; and direct their children.

And let the brightness of the Lord our God be upon us; and direct thou the works of our hands upon us; yea, direct thou the work of our hands.

Glory be, &c.

Ant. Remember not.

Lord, have mercy.

Christ, have mercy.

Lord, have mercy.

Our Father (*in secret*).

V. And lead us not into temptation.

R. But deliver us from evil.

V. Deal favourably, O Lord, in thy good will with Sion.

R. That the walls of Jerusalem may be built up.

V. Then shalt thou accept the sacrifice of justice, oblations, and whole burnt offerings.

R. Then shall they lay calves upon thine altar.

V. Convert us, O Lord God of hosts.

R. And show thy face, and we shall be saved.

V. Convert us, O Lord, and we shall be converted.

R. Renew our days, as from the beginning.

V. O Lord, hear my prayer.

R. And let my cry come unto thee.

Let us pray.

O Lord Jesus Christ, infinite goodness, who, by the divine Sacrament of thy Body and Blood, dost refresh, comfort, and nourish thy Church, and daily offerest thyself a sacrifice of praise and propitiation to the eternal Father; look graciously upon our beloved country, shut out from the sweet delights of this banquet; mercifully pardon all that hath been done or said, through impiety or ignorance, against these most holy mysteries in this land; inspire the minds of all men with faith and reverence for them, that they may become thy children, and be as olive plants round about thy table. Who livest and reignest, world without end. Amen.

Then are said the prayers at the end.

FRIDAY.

From Ps. lxxvi. lxxviii.

I cried unto the Lord with my voice; unto God with my voice, and he hearkened unto me.

In the day of my trouble I sought after God, with my hands in the night lifted up to him; and I was not deceived.

34 DEVOTIONS.

I thought upon the days of old; and I had in my mind the eternal years.

Will God then cast off for ever? or will he never be more favourable again?

Or will he cut off his mercy for ever, from generation to generation?

Or will God forget to show mercy? or will he shut up his mercies in his anger?

And I said, Now have I begun; this is the change of the right hand of the Most High.

Remember not our former iniquities; let thy mercies speedily prevent us, for we are become exceeding poor.

Help us, O God, our Saviour, and for the glory of thy name, O Lord, deliver us; and be merciful unto our sins for thy name's sake.

But we that are thy people, and the sheep of thy pasture, will give thanks unto thee for ever.

We will show forth thy praise unto generation and generation.

Glory be, &c.

Ant. Remember not.

Lord, have mercy.

Christ, have mercy.

Lord, have mercy.

Our Father (*in secret*).

V. And lead us not into temptation.

R. But deliver us from evil.

V. The Lord buildeth up Jerusalem.

R. He will gather together the dispersed of Israel.

V. He hath remembered his mercy.

R. And his truth toward the house of Israel.

V. Convert us, O Lord God of hosts.

R. And show thy face, and we shall be saved.

V. Convert us, O Lord, and we shall be converted.

R. Renew our days, as from the beginning.

V. O Lord, hear my prayer.

R. And let my cry come unto thee.

Let us pray.

O God, who, building thy Church with infinite wisdom, didst hew out seven pillars, instituting the seven sacraments of the new law, whereby the souls of thy faithful are cleansed from sin, strengthened for combat, and trained unto life eternal;

look graciously upon our beloved country, sinking under the want of so many heavenly blessings ; that, the springs of this sevenfold grace being opened, she may draw waters with joy out of the fountains of the Saviour. Who liveth and reigneth with thee, world without end. Amen.

Then are said the prayers at the end.

SATURDAY.

Ant. Remember not.

From Psalm lxxxviii.

The mercies of the Lord I will sing for ever.

I will show forth thy truth with my mouth to generation and generation.

For thou hast said: Mercy shall be built up for ever in the heavens; thy truth shall be stablished in them.

I have made a covenant with mine elect, I have sworn unto David my servant : Thy seed will I stablish for ever.

But if his children forsake my law, and walk not in my judgments,

I will visit their iniquities with a rod, and their sins with stripes.

But my mercy I will not utterly take from him: neither will I suffer my truth to fail.

But thou hast rejected and despised, thou hast been angry with thine Anointed.

Thou hast overthrown the covenant of thy servant, thou hast profaned his sanctuary on the earth.

Thou hast broken down all his hedges, thou hast turned his stronghold into fear.

Thou hast set up the right hand of them that oppress him, thou hast made all his enemies to rejoice.

Where are thy ancient mercies, O Lord; as thou swarest unto David in thy truth ?

Be mindful, O Lord, of the reproach of thy servants (which I have borne in my bosom) of many nations.

Blessed be the Lord for evermore; so be it, and so be it.

Glory be, &c.

Ant. Remember not.
Lord, have mercy.
Christ, have mercy.

Lord, have mercy.

Our Father (*in secret*).

V. Lead us not into temptation.

R. But deliver us from evil.

V. When the Lord turned again the captivity of Sion.

R. We became like men that are comforted.

V. The Lord hath done great things for us.

R. We are become very joyful.

V. Convert us, O Lord God of hosts.

R. And show thy face, and we shall be saved.

V. Convert us, O Lord, and we shall be converted.

R. Renew our days, as from the beginning.

V. O Lord, hear my prayer.

R. And let my cry come unto thee.

Let us pray.

O most loving Lord Jesus, who, hanging on the Cross, didst commend us all, in the person of thy disciple John, to thy most sweet Mother, that we might find in her our refuge, our solace, and our hope; look graciously upon our beloved country, bereaved of so powerful a patronage; that, acknowledging once more the dignity of this most holy Virgin, it may honour and venerate her with all affection of devotion, and own her as Queen and Mother. May her sweet name be lisped by little ones, and linger on the lips of the aged and the dying;—may it be invoked by the afflicted and hymned by the joyful, that this Star of the Sea, being their protection and their guide, all may come to the harbour of eternal salvation. Who livest and reignest world without end. Amen.

Then are said the following prayers.

To beg the Prayers of the Saints.

O merciful God, let the glorious intercession of thy Saints assist us; particularly the most Blessed Virgin Mary, Mother of thy only-begotten Son, and thy holy Apostles, Peter and Paul, to whose patronage we humbly recommend our most beloved country. Be mindful of our fathers, Gregory, Bishop of the holy city, and Augustine, who delivered to us inviolate the faith of the holy Roman Church. Remember our holy martyrs, who shed their blood for Christ; but especially thy most glorious Bishop, Thomas. Remember all those holy confessors, bishops, and kings, all those monks and hermits, all those holy virgins and widows, who made this once the Island of Saints, illustrious by their glorious merits and virtues. Let not their memory perish from before thee, O Lord, but let their supplication enter daily into thy sight; and do thou, who didst so often spare thy sinful people for the sake of Abraham, Isaac, and Jacob, now also, moved by the prayers of our fathers reigning with thee, have mercy upon us, save thy people, and bless thine inheritance; and suffer not those souls to perish which thy Son hath redeemed with his most precious blood. Who liveth and reigneth with thee, world without end. Amen.

ROSARY OF THE MOST BLESSED VIRGIN MARY.

THE FIVE JOYFUL MYSTERIES.

I. *The Annunciation.*

Let us contemplate, in this mystery, how the Angel Gabriel saluted our Blessed Lady with the title, 'Full of Grace,' and declared unto her the Incarnation of our Lord and Saviour Jesus Christ.

Our Father. Ten Hail Marys. Glory be to the Father, &c.

Let us pray.

O holy Mary, Queen of Virgins, through the most high mystery of the Incarnation of thy beloved Son, our Lord Jesus Christ, wherein our salvation was begun, obtain for us, through thy most holy intercession, light to understand the greatness of the benefit he hath bestowed upon us, in vouchsafing to become our Brother, and giving thee, his own beloved Mother, to be our Mother also. Amen.

II. *The Visitation.*

Let us contemplate, in this mystery, how the Blessed Virgin Mary, understanding from the angel that her cousin St. Elisa-

D

beth had conceived, went with haste into the mountains of Judea to visit her, bearing her Divine Son within her womb, and remained with her three months.

Our Father.   Ten Hail Marys.   Glory, &c.

Let us pray.

O holy Virgin, most spotless mirror of humility, by that exceeding charity which moved thee to visit thy holy cousin St. Elisabeth, obtain for us, through thine intercession, that our hearts being visited by thy Divine Son, and freed from all sin, we may praise and give thanks to him for ever.   Amen.

III. *The Birth of our Saviour Christ in Bethlehem.*

Let us contemplate, in this mystery, how the Blessed Virgin Mary, when the time of her delivery was come, brought forth our Redeemer, Jesus Christ, at midnight, and laid him in a manger, because there was no room for him in the inns at Bethlehem.

Our Father.   Ten Hail Marys.   Glory, &c.

Let us pray.

O most pure Mother of God, through thy virginal and most joyful delivery, whereby thou gavest to the world thy only Son, our Saviour, we beseech thee obtain for us, through thine intercession, the grace to lead such pure and holy lives in this world, that we may become worthy to sing, without ceasing, the mercies of thy Son, and his benefits to us by thee.   Amen.

IV. *The Presentation of our Blessed Lord in the Temple.*

Let us contemplate, in this mystery, how the Blessed Virgin Mary, on the day of her purification, presented the child Jesus in the Temple, where holy Simeon, giving thanks to God, with great devotion received him into his arms.

Our Father.   Ten Hail Marys.   Glory, &c.

Let us pray.

O holy Virgin, most admirable mistress and pattern of obedience, who didst present the Lord of the Temple in the Temple of God, obtain for us, of thy Blessed Son, that, with holy Simeon and devout Anna, we may praise and glorify him for ever.   Amen.

V. *The Finding of the Child Jesus in the Temple.*

Let us contemplate, in this mystery, how the Blessed Virgin Mary, after having lost (through no fault of hers) her beloved Son in Jerusalem, sought him for the space of three days, and at length found him in the Temple, sitting in the midst of the doctors, hearing them, and asking them questions, being of the age of twelve years.

Our Father. Ten Hail Marys. Glory, &c.

Let us pray.

O most blessed Virgin, more than martyr in thy sufferings, and yet the comfort of such as are afflicted; by that unspeakable joy wherewith thy soul was filled, when at length thou didst find thy well-beloved Son in the Temple, teaching in the midst of the doctors; obtain of him that we may so seek him and find him in his holy Catholic Church, as never more to be separated from him. Amen.

Salve Regina, &c., Hail, holy Queen, &c. ; with *V.* and *R.* ; and prayer, 'Hear, O merciful God,' &c. ; or else, 'O God, whose only-begotten Son,' &c.

THE FIVE SORROWFUL MYSTERIES.

I. *The Prayer and Bloody Sweat of our Blessed Saviour in Garden.*

Let us contemplate, in this mystery, how our Lord Jesus was so afflicted for us in the garden of Gethsemane, that his body was bathed in a bloody sweat, which ran down in great drops to the ground.

Our Father. Ten Hail Marys. Glory, &c.

Let us pray.

O most holy Virgin, more than martyr; by that ardent prayer which our beloved Saviour poured forth to his Heavenly Father in the garden, vouchsafe to intercede for us, that, our passions being reduced to the obedience of reason, we may always, and in all things, conform and subject ourselves to the holy will of God. Amen.

II. *The Scourging of our Blessed Lord at the Pillar.*

Let us contemplate, in this mystery, how our Lord Jesus Christ was most cruelly scourged in Pilate's house, the number of stripes they gave him being about five thousand.

Our Father.   Ten Hail Marys.   Glory, &c.

Let us pray.

O Mother of God, overflowing fountain of patience, through those stripes thy only and much-beloved Son vouchsafed to suffer for us, obtain of him for us grace to mortify our rebellious senses, to avoid the occasion of sin, and to be ready to suffer everything rather than offend God.   Amen.

III. *The Crowning of our Blessed Saviour with Thorns.*

Let us contemplate, in this mystery, how those cruel ministers of Satan platted a crown of sharp thorns, and cruelly pressed it on the sacred head of our Lord Jesus Christ.

Our Father.   Ten Hail Marys.   Glory, &c.

Let us pray.

O Mother of our Eternal Prince, the King of Glory; by those sharp thorns wherewith his sacred head was pierced, we beseech thee obtain, through thy intercession, that we may be delivered from all motions of pride, and escape that shame which our sins deserve at the day of judgment.   Amen.

IV. *Jesus carrying his Cross.*

Let us contemplate, in this mystery, how our Lord Jesus Christ, being sentenced to die, bore, with the most amazing patience, the Cross which was laid upon him for his greater torment and ignominy.

Our Father.   Ten Hail Marys.   Glory, &c.

Let us pray.

O holy Virgin, example of patience; by the most painful carrying of the Cross, in which thy Son, our Lord Jesus Christ, bore the heavy weight of our sins, obtain for us of him, through thine intercession, courage and strength to follow his steps, and bear our cross after him to the end of our lives.   Amen.

V. *The Crucifixion of our Lord Jesus Christ.*

Let us contemplate, in this mystery, how our Lord Jesus Christ, being come to Mount Calvary, was stripped of his clothes, and his hands and feet nailed to the Cross, in the presence of his most afflicted Mother.

Our Father. Ten Hail Marys. Glory, &c.

Let us pray.

O holy Mary, Mother of God; as the body of thy beloved Son was for us stretched upon the Cross, so may we offer up our souls and bodies to be crucified with him, and our hearts to be pierced with grief at his most bitter Passion; and thou, O most sorrowful Mother, graciously vouchsafe to help us, by thy all-powerful intercession, to accomplish the work of our salvation. Amen.

Salve Regina, or Hail, holy Queen, &c.

Prayer. Hear, O merciful God, &c., or O God, whose only begotten Son, &c.

The Five Glorious Mysteries.

I. *The Resurrection of our Lord from the Dead.*

Let us contemplate, in this mystery, how our Lord Jesus Christ, triumphing gloriously over death, rose again the third day, immortal and impassible.

Our Father. Ten Hail Marys. Glory, &c.

Let us pray.

O glorious Virgin Mary; by that unspeakable joy thou didst receive in the resurrection of thy Divine Son, we beseech thee obtain for us of him, that our hearts may never go astray after the false joys of this world, but may be for ever wholly employed in the pursuit of the only true and solid joys of heaven. Amen.

II. *The Ascension of Christ into Heaven.*

Let us contemplate, in this mystery, how our Lord Jesus Christ, forty days after his resurrection, ascended into heaven, attended by angels, in the sight and to the great admiration of his most holy Mother, and his holy Apostles and disciples.

Our Father. Ten Hail Marys. Glory, &c.

Let us pray.

O Mother of God, comforter of the afflicted; as thy beloved Son, when he ascended into heaven, lifted up his hands and blessed his Apostles, as he was parted from them; so vouchsafe, most holy Mother, to lift up thy pure hands to him on our behalf, that we may enjoy the benefits of his blessing and of thine, here on earth, and hereafter in heaven. Amen.

III. *The Descent of the Holy Ghost on the Apostles.*

Let us contemplate, in this mystery, how the Lord Jesus Christ, being seated on the right hand of God, sent, as he had promised, the Holy Ghost upon his Apostles, who, after he was ascended, returning to Jerusalem, continued in prayer and supplication with the Blessed Virgin Mary, expecting the performance of his promise.

Our Father. Ten Hail Marys. Glory, &c.

Let us pray.

O sacred Virgin, tabernacle of the Holy Ghost; we beseech thee obtain, by thine intercession, that this most sweet Comforter, whom thy beloved Son sent down upon his Apostles, filling them thereby with spiritual joy, may teach us in this world the true way of salvation, and make us to walk in the way of virtue and good works. Amen.

IV. *The Assumption of the Blessed Virgin Mary into Heaven.*

Let us contemplate, in this mystery, how the glorious Virgin, twelve years after the resurrection of her Son, passed out of this world unto him, and was by him assumed into heaven, accompanied by the holy Angels.

Our Father. Ten Hail Marys. Glory, &c.

Let us pray.

O most prudent Virgin, who, entering the heavenly palaces,

didst fill the angels with joy and man with hope; vouchsafe to intercede for us at the hour of our death, that, being delivered from the illusions and temptations of the devil, we may joyfully and securely pass out of this temporal state, to enjoy the happiness of eternal life. Amen.

V. *The Coronation of the most Blessed Virgin Mary in Heaven.*

Let us contemplate, in this mystery, how the glorious Virgin Mary was, to the great jubilee and exultation of the whole court of heaven, and particular glory of all the Saints, crowned by her Son with the brightest diadem of glory.

Our Father. Ten Hail Marys. Glory, &c.

Let us pray.

O glorious Queen of all the heavenly host; we beseech thee accept this Rosary, which, as a crown of roses, we offer at thy feet; and grant, most gracious Lady, that, by thy intercession, our souls may be inflamed with so ardent a desire of seeing thee so gloriously crowned, that it may never die within us, until it shall be changed into the happy fruition of thy blessed sight. Amen.

Salve Regina, or Hail, holy Queen, &c.

Prayer. Hear, O merciful God, &c., or O God, whose only-begotten Son, &c.

O, Cor amoris, Victima
Cœli perenne gaudium,
Mortalium solatium,
Mortalium spes ultima.

Cor dulce, Cor amabile,
Amore nostri saucium,

Amore nostri languidum,
Fac sis mihi placabile.

Jesu! Patris cor unicum,
Puris amicum mentibus,
Puris amandum cordibus
In corde regnes omnium.

Amen.

Cor Jesu.

To Jesus' Heart, all burning
  With fervent love for men,
My heart with fondest yearning
  Shall raise its joyful strain.

CHORUS.

While ages course along,
Blest be with loudest song
The Sacred Heart of Jesus
By every heart and tongue.

O Heart, for sinners riven
  By sheer excess of love,
The spear through thee was
    driven,
  'Twas sin of mine that drove.

O Heart, for me on fire
  With love no tongue can
    speak,
My yet untold desire
  God gives me for thy sake.

Dear Lord, my soul would ven-
    ture
  To urge one earnest prayer:
Keep, Lord, in thy Heart's cen-
    tre
  One little nook for her.

Too true I have forsaken
  Thy hearth by wilful sin;

Yet let me now be taken
  Back to my home again.

From all that can infect me,
  O cleanse me with thy blood;
For thine own spouse elect me,
  My God, my Sovereign Good!

As thou art meek and lowly,
  And ever pure of heart,
So may my heart be wholly
  Of thine the counterpart.

Away with earthly passion,
  Away with sordid pelf;
In my heart's consecration,
  I yield thee all myself.

Would that to me were given
  The pinions of the dove!
I'd pierce the highest heaven
  My Jesus' love to prove.

Within the cleft I'll cower
  Of Jesus' wounded side;
In sunshine or in shower,
  Securely there I'll hide.

When life away is flying,
  And earth's false glare is
    done,
Still, Sacred Heart, in dying,
  I'll say, 'I'm all thine own.'

Veni Creator Spiritus,
Mentes tuorum visita,

Imple superna gratia,

Quæ tu creasti pectora.

Come, O Creator Spirit blest,
And in our souls take up thy
    rest;
Come, with thy grace and hea-
    venly aid,   [hast made.
To fill the hearts which thou

Qui diceris Paraclitus,
Altissimi donum Dei,
Fons vivus, ignis, charitas,
Et spiritalis unctio.

Great Paraclete, to thee we cry;
O highest gift of God most high!
O fount of life! O fire of love!
And sweet anointing from a-
bove.

Tu septiformis munere,

Thou in thy sevenfold gifts art
known; [own;
The finger of God's hand we
The promise of the Father thou,
Who dost the tongue with power
endow.

Digitus Paternæ dexteræ,
Tu rite promissum Patris,
Sermone ditans guttura.

Accende lumen sensibus,
Infunde amorem cordibus,

Kindle our senses from above,
And make our hearts o'erflow
with love; [high,
With patience firm, and virtue
The weakness of our flesh sup-
ply.

Infirma nostri corporis
Virtute firmans perpeti.

Hostem repellas longius,

Far from us drive the foe we
dread, [instead;
And grant us thy true peace
So shall we not, with thee for
guide,
Turn from the path of life aside.

Pacemque dones protinus;
Ductore sic te prævio

Vitemus omne noxium.

Per te sciamus da Patrem,
Noscamus atque Filium,

O may thy grace on us bestow
The Father and the Son to
know, [confess'd
And thee through endless times
Of both th' eternal Spirit blest.

Teque utriusque Spiritum
Credamus omni tempore.

Deo Patri sit gloria,
Et Filio, qui a mortuis
Surrexit, ac Paraclito,

All glory while the ages run
Be to the Father, and the Son
Who rose from death; the same
to thee,
O Holy Ghost, eternally.

In sæculorum sæcula.
Amen.

Amen.

Jesus, my Lord, my God, my all.

Jesus, my Lord, my God, my
    all;
  How can I love thee as I
    ought,
And how revere this wondrous
    gift,
  So far surpassing hope or
    thought?
    Sweet Sacrament, we thee
      adore;
    O make us love thee more
      and more.

Had I but Mary's sinless heart
  To love thee with, my dear-
    est King;
O, with what bursts of fervent
    praise
  Thy goodness, Jesus, would
    I sing!
    Sweet Sacrament, &c.

O, see, within a creature's
    hand   [be,
  The vast Creator deigns to
Reposing   infant - like,   as
    though
  On Joseph's arm, or Mary's
    knee.
    Sweet Sacrament, &c.

Thy Body, Soul, and Godhead,
    all,—
  O mystery of love divine!—
I cannot compass all I have,
  For all thou hast and art
    are mine.
    Sweet Sacrament, &c.

Sound,   sound   his   praises
    higher still,
  And come, ye Angels, to our
    aid;   [God,
'Tis God, 'tis God, the very
  Whose power both man and
    angels made.
    Sweet Sacrament, &c.

(For Processions.)

Ring joyously, ye solemn bells,
  And wave, O wave, ye cen-
    sers bright;
'Tis Jesus cometh, Mary's Son,
  And God of God and Light
    of light.
    Sweet Sacrament, &c.

O earth, grow flowers beneath
    his feet;
  And thou, O sun, shine
    bright this day;
He comes, he comes, O heaven
    on earth,
  Our Jesus comes upon his
    way.
    Sweet Sacrament, &c.

He comes, he comes, the Lord
    of Hosts,
  Borne on his throne trium-
    phantly;
We see thee, and we know
    thee, Lord;
  And yearn to shed our blood
    for thee.
    Sweet Sacrament, &c.

Our hearts leap up; our trem-
bling song
Grows fainter still; we can
no more ;   [die
Silence, and let us weep, and

Of very love, while we adore.
Great Sacrament of love
divine,
All, all we have or are be
thine.

Immaculate, Immaculate !

O Mother, I could weep for
mirth,
Joy fills my heart so fast ;
My soul to-day is heaven on
earth ;
O, could the transport last !
I think of thee, and what thou
Thy majesty, thy state, [art,
And I keep singing, in my heart,
Immaculate, immaculate !

When Jesus looks upon thy
face,
His heart with rapture glows;
And in the Church, by his sweet
grace,
Thy blessed worship grows.
I think of thee, &c.

The angels answer with their
songs,
Bright choirs in gleaming
rows ;
And saints flock round thy feet
in throngs,
And heaven with bliss o'er-
flows.
I think of thee, &c.

Immaculate Conception ! far
Above all graces blest ;
Thou shinest like a royal star
On God's eternal breast.
I think of thee, &c.

God bless our Pope !

Full in the panting heart of
Rome,   [dome,
Beneath th' Apostles' crowning
From pilgrims' lips that kiss the
ground,   [sound—
Breathes in all tongues one only
God bless our Pope, the great,
the good !

The golden roof, the marble
walls,
The Vatican's majestic halls,
The note redouble, till it fills
With echoes sweet the Seven
Hills—
God bless our Pope, the great,
the good !

From torrid south to frozen
north [forth,
The wave harmonious stretches
Yet strikes no chord more true
to Rome's [and homes—
Than rings within our hearts
God bless our Pope, the great,
the good!

For, like the sparks of unseen
fire, [wire,
That speak along the magic
From home to home, from heart
to heart, [dren dart—
These words of countless chil-

God bless our Pope, the great,
the good!

To homes and hearts of Saints
above,
Which link'd with ours in
thought and love,
Repeating, bless the pilgrims'
strain, [rowed rain—
As showers enrich with bor-
God bless our Pope, the great,
the good!

Psalm L. *Miserere.*

Miserere mei, Deus : secundum magnam misericordiam tuam.

Et secundum multitudinem miserationum tuarum : dele iniquitatem meam.

Amplius lava me ab iniquitate mea : et a peccato meo munda me.

Quoniam iniquitatem meam ego cognosco : et peccatum meum contra me est semper.

Tibi soli peccavi, et malum coram te feci : ut justificeris in sermonibus tuis, et vincas cum judicaris.

Ecce enim in iniquitatibus conceptus sum : et in peccatis concepit me mater mea.

1 Have mercy upon me, O God : according to thy great mercy.

2 And according to the multitude of thy tender mercies : blot out my iniquity.

3 Wash me yet more from my iniquity : and cleanse me from my sin.

4 For I acknowledge my iniquity : and my sin is always before me.

5 Against thee only have I sinned, and done evil in thy sight : that thou mayest be justified in thy words, and mayest overcome when thou art judged.

6 For behold, I was conceived in iniquities : and in sins did my mother conceive me.

Ecce enim veritatem dilexisti : incerta et occulta sapientiæ tuæ manifestasti mihi.

Asperges me hyssopo, et mundabor : lavabis me, et super nivem dealbabor.

Auditui meo dabis gaudium et lætitiam : et exultabunt ossa humiliata.

Averte faciem tuam a peccatis meis : et omnes iniquitates meas dele.

Cor mundum crea in me, Deus : et spiritum rectum innova in visceribus meis.

Ne projicias me a facie tua : et Spiritum Sanctum tuum ne auferas a me.

Redde mihi lætitiam salutaris tui : et spiritu principali confirma me.

Docebo iniquos vias tuas : et impii ad te convertentur.

Libera me de sanguinibus, Deus, Deus salutis meæ : et exultabit lingua mea justitiam tuam.

Domine, labia mea aperies : et os meum annuntiabit laudem tuam.

Quoniam si voluisses sacrificium, dedissem utique : holocaustis non delectaberis.

7 For behold, thou hast loved truth : the uncertain and hidden things of thy wisdom thou hast made manifest unto me.

8 Thou shalt sprinkle me with hyssop, and I shall be cleansed : thou shalt wash me, and I shall be made whiter than snow.

9 Thou shalt make me hear of joy and gladness : and the bones that were humbled shall rejoice.

10 Turn away thy face from my sins : and blot out all my iniquities.

11 Create in me a clean heart, O God : and renew a right spirit within my bowels.

12 Cast me not away from thy presence : and take not thy Holy Spirit from me.

13 Restore unto me the joy of thy salvation : and strengthen me with a perfect spirit.

14 I will teach the unjust thy ways : and the wicked shall be converted unto thee.

15 Deliver me from bloodguiltiness, O God, thou God of my salvation : and my tongue shall extol thy justice.

16 Thou shalt open my lips, O Lord : and my mouth shall declare thy praise.

17 For if thou hadst desired sacrifice, I would surely have given it : with burnt-offerings thou wilt not be delighted.

Sacrificium Deo spiritus contribulatus : cor contritum et humiliatum, Deus, non despicies.

Benigne fac, Domine, in bona voluntate tua Sion : ut ædificentur muri Jerusalem.

Tunc acceptabis sacrificium justitiæ, oblationes, et holocausta : tunc imponent super altare tuum vitulos.

Gloria, &c.

18 The sacrifice of God is an afflicted spirit : a contrite and humble heart, O God, thou wilt not despise.

19 Deal favourably, O Lord, in thy good will with Sion : that the walls of Jerusalem may be built up.

20 Then shalt thou accept the sacrifice of justice, oblations, and whole burnt-offerings : then shall they lay calves upon thine altars.

Glory, &c.

———

Te Deum.

Te Deum laudamus : te Dominum confitemur.

Te æternum Patrem : omnis terra veneratur.

Tibi omnes angeli : tibi cœli et universæ potestates ;

Tibi cherubim et seraphim : incessabili voce proclamant ;

Sanctus, sanctus, sanctus : Dominus Deus Sabaoth.

Pleni sunt cœli et terra : majestatis gloriæ tuæ.

Te gloriosus : Apostolorum chorus.

Te Prophetarum : laudabilis numerus.

Te Martyrum : candidatus laudat exercitus.

We praise thee, O God : we acknowledge thee to be the Lord.

All the earth doth worship thee : the Father everlasting.

To thee all angels : to thee the heavens and all the powers therein ;

To thee cherubim and seraphim : continually cry ;

Holy, holy, holy : Lord God of Sabaoth.

Heaven and earth are full : of the majesty of thy glory.

The glorious choir of the Apostles.

The admirable company of the Prophets.

The white-robed army of Martyrs : praise thee.

Te per orbem terrarum: sancta confitetur Ecclesia.

Patrem: immensæ majestatis.

: Venerandum tuum verum: et unicum Filium.

Sanctum quoque: Paraclitum Spiritum.

Tu Rex gloriæ: Christe.

Tu Patris : sempiternus es Filius.

Tu ad liberandum suscepturus hominem : non horruisti Virginis uterum.

Tu devicto mortis aculeo : aperuisti credentibus regna cœlorum.

Tu ad dexteram Dei sedes : in gloria Patris.

· Judex crederis: esse venturus.

* Te ergo quæsumus, tuis famulis subveni : quos pretioso sanguine redemisti.

Æterna fac cum Sanctis tuis : in gloria numerari.

Salvum fac populum tuum, Domine: et benedic hæreditati tuæ.

Et rege eos : et extolle illos usque in æternum.

The Holy Church throughout all the world : doth confess thee.

The Father : of infinite majesty.

Thy adorable, true : and only Son.

Also the Holy Ghost : the Comforter.

Thou art the King of Glory: O Christ.

Thou art the everlasting Son : of the Father.

When thou tookest upon thee to deliver man: thou didst not abhor the Virgin's womb.

When thou hadst overcome the sting of death : thou didst open the kingdom of heaven to all believers.

Thou sittest at the right hand of God : in the glory of the Father.

We believe that thou shalt come : to be our Judge.

We pray thee, therefore, help thy servants : whom thou hast redeemed with thy precious blood.

Make them to be numbered with thy Saints : in glory everlasting.

O Lord, save thy people : and bless thine inheritance.

And govern them : and lift them up for ever.

* Here it is usual to kneel.

Per singulos dies : benedicimus te.

Day by day : we bless thee.

Et laudamus nomen tuum in sæculum : et in sæculum sæculi.

And we praise thy name for ever : yea, for ever and ever.

Dignare, Domine, die isto : sine peccato nos custodire.

Vouchsafe, O Lord, this day: to keep us without sin.

Miserere nostri, Domine : miserere nostri.

O Lord, have mercy upon us : have mercy upon us.

Fiat misericordia tua, Domine, super nos: quemadmodum speravimus in te.

O Lord, let thy mercy be showed upon us : as we have hoped in thee.

In te, Domine, speravi : non confundar in æternum.

O Lord, in thee have I hoped : let me not be confounded for ever.

Faith of our Fathers.

Faith of our fathers, living still,
　In spite of dungeon, fire, and sword;
O, how our hearts beat high with joy
　Whene'er we hear that glorious word!
Faith of our fathers, holy Faith,
We will be true to thee till death.

Our fathers chain'd in prisons dark
　Were still in heart and conscience free;
How sweet would be their children's fate,
　If they, like them, could die for thee!
Faith of our fathers, holy Faith,
We will be true to thee till death.

Faith of our fathers! Mary's prayers
　Shall win our country back to thee;
And through the truth that comes from God,
　O, then indeed we shall be free.
Faith of our fathers, holy Faith,
We will be true to thee till death.

Faith of our fathers, we will love
　Both friend and foe in all our strife,
And preach thee too, as love knows how
　By kindly words and virtuous life.
Faith of our fathers, holy Faith,
We will be true to thee till death.

Daily, daily sing to Mary.

Daily, daily sing to Mary,
　Sing, my soul, her praises due ;
All her feasts, her actions worship
　With the heart's devotion true.
Lost in wond'ring contemplation
　Be her majesty confest :
Call her Mother, call her Virgin,
　Happy Mother, Virgin blest.

She is mighty to deliver ;
　Call her, trust her lovingly :
When the tempest rages round thee
　She will calm the troubled sea.
Gifts of Heaven she has given,
　Noble Lady, to our race ;
She, the Queen, who decks her subjects
　With the light of God's own grace.

All my senses, heart, affections,
　Strive to sound her glory forth ;
Spread abroad the sweet memorials
　Of the Virgin's priceless worth.
Sing in songs of praise unending,
　Sing the world's majestic Queen ;
Weary not, nor faint in telling
　All the gifts she gives to men.

Pilgrimage Hymn.

O Jesus! Lord of life and light!
　　God of all love and boundless power!
'O light in darkness, joy in grief!'
　　Smile on us, Lord, in this thine hour.

From our own sea-girt Isle we come—
　　The Isle of Saints in days of yore—
Faith's pilgrim sons, we cross the main,
　　The Heart of Jesus to adore.

That sacred Heart on every breast
　　Tells of the love that burns within,
For Him who showed that Heart of his,
　　These hardened hearts of ours to win.

High let it wave, that badge divine,
　　The Pilgrim's banner raise aloft,
Its flutter speaks of him whose voice
　　'Has still'd an angry world so oft.'

O, by the words of sweetest power
　　Thou erst didst speak in Paray's walls,
And every spell whose lingering grace
　　On listening heart and spirit falls;

By every hope that leads us on;
　　By every pledge in mercy given,—
Hear, Lord, the English Pilgrim's prayer;
　　Throw open wide the gates of Heaven!

Send down thy grace in bounteous streams,
　　Rain on us all thy choicest gifts;
Patience and love and faith, whose strength
　　Mountains of mighty weight uplifts.

Yet once more speak the words which turn
　　Darkness to light—O, let light shine
On that dear country, those dear homes
　　Which once, O dearest Lord, were thine.

' We love to kiss each print where thou
    Hast left the mark of thy dear feet ;'
We love to kneel on every spot
    Where traces of thy love we meet.

O, turn thy steps, O, show thy Heart
    To England once so dear to thee ;
Give to her Pilgrims, one and all,
    Heralds of love and peace to be.

Yet one more prayer, one louder cry,
    Than e'en for kindred or for home,
We raise, O God, for him who mourns
    O'er thine own fallen city, Rome !

The captive lord of countless hearts,
    The Father and the Pontiff King,
Beneath whose sway we love to lie
    As children 'neath a mother's wing.

And as we tread a foreign soil,
    And catch the oft-repeated strain
That floats along the lucid air
    That hovers o'er the sunlit plain,

Let heart and voice join in the prayer
    That swells the breeze for Peter's dome :
' O, by thy Heart, thy Sacred Heart,
    Jesus, save England, France, and Rome !'

THE END.

BOOKS PUBLISHED

BY

MESSRS. BURNS AND OATES.

————o————

THE TWO-SHILLING UNIVERSAL PRAYER-BOOK.

THE PATH TO HEAVEN;

The Cheapest and most Complete Book of Devotions for Public or Private use ever issued.   (25th Thousand.)

UPWARDS OF ONE THOUSAND PAGES FOR TWO SHILLINGS.

————————

It contains :

1. All the usual Devotions for Morning and Evening, Prayers at Mass, for Confession, Communion, the Sacraments, the Sick, &c.

2. Litanies, Novenas, Devotions, and Hymns, in regular order, *for every month in the year* (including Indulgenced Prayers), intended for use in Evening Services in Churches, as well as in private. This is an *entirely novel feature*, and will, it is presumed, make the Volume a *sine quâ non* in every Mission.

3. Offices : besides Vespers, Compline, Office of Immaculate Conception, &c., it comprises the " Bona Mors," Novena of St. Francis Xavier, and Sacred-Heart Devotions, used by the Jesuit Fathers ; the Holy-Family Devotions ; the Devotions for the Precious Blood ; also Meditations, and the EPISTLES AND GOSPELS for the Year.

4. The most copious and varied collection of *Hymns and Sacred Songs* hitherto published (293).   Music, 1*s.*

Price:

Cloth lettered, Two Shillings.		Morocco, gilt	7s.	0d.
Neatly bound, red edges	2s. 6d.	Morocco, gilt extra	8	0
Roan, lettered	3 0	Morocco, gilt, rim and clasp	14	0
Cloth, rims & bar, red edges	4 0	Velvet, rim and clasp	10	6
Roan, richly gilt and clasp	4 6	Best Turkey morocco	8	6
French morocco, gilt edges	4 0	Best Turkey morocco, gilt	10	0
Calf, red edges	5 0	Ivory	12	0
Best calf	7 6	Ditto, best ornamented	42	0
Morocco	6 0	Best Velvet, rim and clasp	30	0

The Imitation of the Sacred Heart. By the Rev. Fr. ARNOLD, S.J. Translated by a Father of the same Company. 12mo, 4s. 6d.; or in handsome cloth, red edges, 5s. Also, calf, 8s. 6d.; morocco, 9s. 6d.; ditto, very neat, with edges turned over, 13s.

Approved (in a letter to the Author) by Father ROOTHAN, General of the Society of Jesus, and by four Theological Censors.

"Of all the books which we have seen on this Devotion, it is at once the most solidly practical and the most fervently devotional."—*Dublin Review.*

The New Month of Mary; or the Second Eve. By the Right Rev. Bishop DECHAMPS, of Namur. Translated by the Author of the "Life of St. Theresa," &c. &c. Cloth, 3s.

The See of St. Peter. With reference to Dr. Pusey's "Eirenicon." By T. W. ALLIES, M.A., author of "The Formation of Christendom," &c. New edition, 4s. 6d.

The Popular Choir Manual. A Cheap Collection of easy and attractive Catholic Music for Morning and Evening Services during the whole course of the Ecclesiastical Year. Morning, 3s. 6d.; Evening, 5s. 6d.; or in one vol. 10s. 6d.

This work carries on and completes the plan of "Webbe's Motetts" and other works of the kind, which are found inadequate to modern requirements.

Hymns for the Year, containing also Benediction and other Latin Pieces in general use. This is *the cheapest and most complete Hymn-Book ever issued.* It contains not only the favourite Hymns from the Oratory and other Catholic Hymnals, but also many new and beautiful Hymns and Sacred Songs by St. Alphonsus, &c. Price 3d. Also, very strong cloth, 5d.

HYMNS FOR THE YEAR, with PUBLIC DEVOTIONS for every Evening. 6d.

HYMNS FOR THE YEAR, bound with the VESPER-BOOK, 6d.; or in strong cloth, 1s. The most complete and cheap book of the kind.

THE MUSIC-BOOK of 244 Melodies for "Hymns for the Year," the Oratory, and all other Hymn-Books, &c. 1s.

Vocal Parts and Accompaniments to the above in

THE POPULAR HYMN AND TUNE BOOK

For one, two, three, and four Voices, with Accompaniment; containing a large variety of Hymns and Sacred Songs for general use, and for every occasion throughout the year; together with a number of Easy Melodies suited for Schools and elementary use. Edited by FREDERICK WESTLAKE, Associate of the Royal Academy of Music. One handsome volume, cloth, 10s. 6d., or in Three Parts at 3s. each.

*** *The style and arrangement of this Collection render it especially useful not only for public use, but also in Convent and other Schools, now that vocal music is generally made an essential part of the educational course.*

Life of the Curé d'Ars. From the French. With Preface by Right Rev. Dr. MANNING. New edition, enlarged. 4s.

The New School and College History of England.
One volume, large post 8vo, 820 pp., cloth, 6s.

True Devotion to the Blessed Virgin. By the Ven.
GRIGNON DE MONTFORT. Translated, with a Preface,
by the Very Rev. Dr. FABER. Blue cloth, neat, 2s. 6d.

Hymns and Sacred Verses, from the Italian of St.
ALPHONSUS. Neat pocket size, cloth, 1s.
N.B.—Music for these Hymns contained in the "Hymns
and Melodies for the Year," 1s.

The Prayers of St. Gertrude and St. Mechtilde.
Now first translated from the original Latin. Beautifully printed in a Pocket size. Neat cloth, lettered,
1s. 6d.; French morocco, red edges, 2s.; best calf, red
edges, 4s. 6d.; best morocco, plain, 5s.; gilt, 6s. On
thin *vellum paper* at the same prices. *Common paper*
edition at 1s.

Also,
The Exercises of St. Gertrude. A companion volume,
at same prices.

Fioretti; or the Flowers of St. Francis of Assisi.
Translated from the Italian. Fcp. 8vo, 3s.

Sister Emmerich's Meditations on the Passion. Full
edition, fcp. 8vo, cloth, 3s. 6d.

Flowers of Mary. A Book of Devotion and Meditation
for the course of the Year, with Hymns. By a FRAN-
CISCAN. Fcp. 8vo, neat cloth, 3s.

5

St. Liguori's Preparation for Death. Correct Translation by the REDEMPTORIST FATHERS. New People's Edition. 2*s*.

BOOKS FOR CATHOLIC SCHOOLS.

Primer, with woodcuts. 1½*d*.
Book I. (woodcuts), 2*d*. ; Primer and Book I. together, 4*d*.
Book II. (woodcuts). 5*d*.
Supplement to Book I. (woodcuts). 4*d*.
Supplement to Book II. (woodcuts). 6*d*.
[These Two Books supply the want of additional reading which is often felt in the junior classes. They also comprise elementary lessons in writing and arithmetic.]
Book III., containing more advanced lessons. 8*d*.
Book IV., containing lessons for the higher classes. 1*s*.
The Child's Spelling and Reading Book, 6*d*. ; or, the Two Parts separately, 4*d*. each.
[By means of this Book, with its simple musical notes, and other appliances, children acquire spelling very rapidly and accurately.]
Tablet Lessons, including Alphabet and Figures, in very large type, 1*s*. 6*d*. ; Alphabet and Figure Sheet by itself, 2*d*.
The Pictorial Reading-Book ; many cuts. 1*s*. 4*d*.
The Catechetical Reading-Book for Schools. In Two Parts. Part I. Outlines of Sacred History and Scripture Geography. Part II. Lessons on Doctrinal and Practical Subjects, following the arrangement of the Catechism used in Schools. By the Very Rev. Canon GRIFFIN, Nottingham. Cloth, 1*s*. 4*d*.

A New Historical Catechism. Price 4*d*.
——————— Chart. 2*s*. 6*d*. ; rollers, 5*s*. 6*d*.

Lessons on Christian Doctrine, on a Sheet. 2d.
Catechetical Reading-Book. 1s. 4d.
Full Catechism of the Catholic Religion. By the Rev. J.
  FANDER. Limp, 1s. 6d.; cloth, 2s.
Introduction to the History of England. 1s. 8d.
History of England for Children; Plates. 3s.
History of England for Colleges and Families. 6s.
Catechism of the History of England. 6d.
Manual of Christian Doctrine. 3s.
Manual of Church History. 2s.
Reeve and Challoner's Bible History. 2s.
Prints for ditto, coloured. 16s. and 12s.
Children's Mass-Book for Singing, &c. 1½d.
Old-Testament Stories. 1s. 4d.
Gospel Stories. 1s.
Manual of Confirmation. 2d.
Robinson Crusoe (revised for Catholic Schools). 2s. 6d.
A First Book of Poetry. 1s.
A Second ditto. 2s.
A Third ditto (Selections by De Vere). 3s. 6d.
Sacred Poetry for Schools. Pocket size. 1s.
A Popular History of France. Illustrated. 3s. 6d.
Pocket French Grammar. Cloth, 1s.
Vade Mecum of French Conversation. 1s.
Catechism of English Grammar. Wrapper, 2d.; cloth, 3d.

Burns' Series of New Standard Lesson-Books adapted to the Revised Code of 1871.

BOOK I. adapted to STANDARD 1, 6d.
„ II. „ „ 2, 7d.
„ III. „ „ 3, 10d.
„ IV. „ „ 4, 1s.
„ V. „ „ 5 & 6, 1s. 4d.

Primer, separately (being Part I. of Book I.), 1s. 6d. per doz.
Lesson Sheets of the same, large type, for Schools, 1s. 6d.

Daily Exercise. New edition, with new and superior engravings. Cloth, 6d.; bound and gilt, 1s.

Devotions for the "Quarant' Ore;" or New Visits to the Blessed Sacrament. Edited by Cardinal Wiseman. 1s. 6d., or in cloth, gilt edges, 2s.; morocco, 5s.

Devotions for Country Missions, with full Collection of Hymns. 6d.

Family Prayers, from Catholic Sources, old and new. 2s.

The Spirit of St. Teresa. 2s.; red edges, with Portrait, 2s. 6d.; calf, 5s.; morocco, 5s. 6d.

Spirit of the Curé d'Ars. 2s. Also in various bindings, as "St. Teresa."

Manna of the New Covenant; Devotions for Communion. Cloth, 2s.; bound, with red edges, 2s. 6d.

Manual of the Sacred Heart. New Edition, 2s.; red edges, 2s. 6d.; calf, 5s. 6d.; morocco, 6s. 6d.

A'Kempis. The Following of Christ, in Four Books: a new Translation, beautifully printed in royal 16mo, with borders round each page, and illustrative engravings after designs by the best German artists. Cloth, 3s. 6d.; calf, 7s.; morocco, 8s. 6d.; gilt, 11s.

The same, Pocket Edition. Cloth, 1s.; bound, roan, 1s. 6d.; Fr. morocco, 2s. 6d.; calf, 4s. 6d.; morocco, 5s.; gilt, 6s.

Spiritual Combat; a new and careful Translation. 18mo, cloth, 3*s.* ; calf, 6*s.* ; morocco, 7*s.* ; gilt, 8*s.*
The same, Pocket size. Cloth, 1*s.* ; Fr. morocco, 2*s.* 6*d.* ; calf, neat, 4*s.* ; morocco, 4*s.* 6*d.* ; gilt, 5*s.* 6*d.*

Manual of our Lady of the Sacred Heart. 2*s.* 6*d.*

New Testament. New Pocket Edition, in beautiful type, neat roan, 1*s.* ; embossed, 1*s.* 6*d.* ; Fr. morocco, 3*s.*; gilt, 3*s.* 6*d.* ; calf, 4*s.* 6*d.*; best morocco, 5*s.* ; gilt, 6*s.*

Office of the B.V.M., Latin and English. 6*d.* ; roan, 1*s.* ; calf, 3*s.* 6*d.* ; morocco, 4*s.*

The Psalter in Latin. 1*s.* 6*d.*

Ditto in English. New edition, 2*s.*

Select Offices from the Ritual, Pontifical, and Breviary. Uniformly printed, English and Latin.
The Office of Baptism. 2*d.*
The Office of Burial. 3*d.*
The Order of Laying the Foundation-stone of a Church. 2*d.*
The Rite of Blessing a Bell. 2*d.*
The Offices of Prime and Compline. 8*d.*
The Offices of Tierce, Sext, and None. 3*d.*

The New Testament Narrative, in the Words of the Sacred Writers. With Notes, Chronological Tables, and Maps. Neat cloth, 2*s.*

"The compilers deserve great praise for the manner in which they have performed their task. We commend this little volume as well and carefully printed, and as furnishing its readers, moreover, with a great amount of useful information in the tables inserted at the end."—*Month.*
"It is at once clear, complete, and beautiful."—*Catholic Opinion.*

BURNS & OATES, 17, 18 Portman-street, W.

www.ingramcontent.com/pod-product-compliance
Lightning Source LLC
Chambersburg PA
CBHW020231090426
42735CB00010B/1643